Beyond Rust - Larry Smith

More on *Milltown Natural*

"Looking across my years of friendship with Dick Hague, I see again in these stories all those places and people that never let go of him, nor he of them. They are told from the other side of experience, in ways only life really lived can speak. They are the best of what language can do, looking back toward the reader with a light from within each memory, place, loved one. These stories are a pleasure, rich and alive, every one."
-Joe Enzweiler

"*Milltown Natural* is a book in the American Transcendental tradition. Richard Hague is a true son of Thoreau, for his method is close observation of and meditation on the meanings to be found in the small, the daily, and the otherwise unreported. And, as a true son of Thoreau, he makes his own path; these explorations are enmeshed in, and not in retreat from, the lived networks of neighborhood, class, culture, and the wounded and the interconnected natural environment. These meditations make a fit companion to Richard Hague's fine poetry."
-Michael Henson

BOTTOM DOG PRESS,
c/o Firelands College, Huron, Ohio 44839

The Ohio Arts Council helped fund this program with state tax dollars to encourage economic growth, educational excellence and cultural enrichment for all Ohioans.

Milltown Natural

Essays and Stories
From a Life

1997

Richard Hague

Working Lives Series
Bottom Dog Press
Huron, Ohio

Acknowledgments

I gratefully acknowledge the editors of the following, in which these essays and stories, sometimes in slightly different form, have appeared or been recognized earlier:

Ambergris
"To Live Like An Animal"; Reprinted in *Pine Mt. Sand & Gravel: Contemporary Appalachian Writing*, Volume 4
Appalachian Heritage
"The Line"
Creative Nonfiction
"Menagerie"
Hackberry
"All The Way To China"
Ohio Magazine
"Shitepokes, Night Fish, And The Jumping Buckeyes" (under the title "A Midsummer Night's Stream"), "Small Bright Things, And Flash, And Glint, And Glitter" (under the title "Corrected Vision"), "The Snake Man" (under the title "Snake Eyes"), "Bike" (under the title "Zen And The Art of Motorcylce Construction"), "Mowing The Bald," "A Porch In The Country," "Basement" (under the title "The Sweet Smell of Home"); Reprinted in *In Buckeye Country: Photos and Essays of Ohio Life*, Bottom Dog Press
Soaptown: A Magazine of Cincinnati Writing
"Needles"; "Breaking"; Reprinted in *Getting By: Stories of Working Lives*, eds. David Shevin and Larry Smith, Bottom Dog Press
Syzygy
"Aunt Aggie"; Reprinted in *Ohio Magazine* under title "Closest Kin" and in *Down The River: A Collection of Ohio Valley Fiction and Poetry*, ed. Dallas Wiebe
In addition, "The Snake Man" appears as the end-piece in *Down Home, Downtown: Urban Appalachians Today*, ed. Philip Obermiller.
"Carp, And Other Lessons" was a Finalist in the 1995 New Letters Literary Awards.
A manuscript containing many of the essays herein was a Finalist in the Associated Writing Programs Award in Creative Nonfiction.
Thanks also to Tim Russell.

Milltown Natural

Contents

Part One

Part Two

PART ONE

Ohio River flood, foot of Logan Street, Steubenville, c.1940's
(Hague family photo)

Shitepokes, Nightfish, And
The Jumping Buckeyes

The old characters came with summer. They had names like Kinny Peakskill, General Wiggins, Back Door Dillman. White men and black, slim and paunchy, they chewed Beech Nut or smoked Parodis, Rum Crooks or Marsh Wheeling Stogies. Some of them bore hard white scars as long as snakes on their forearms; some squinted their red-rimmed eyes even when they stood in the shade of the willows. None talked freely to strangers, but occasionally, I could hear them singing as they hoed their long rows down by the river.

They were big men, rough-hewn and cursing, different from my uncles who worked uptown in the high gray buildings or the mills. These men knew little of legal briefs or open hearths, but they could get the mud-vein out of a carp. They could skin a catfish quick. They knew how to drink hard liquor. In the late days of August, sweating and grunting, they hauled load after load of watermelons up Logan Street. Later, after the first frost struck, I could walk along the tracks and smell the rotting leaves and vines, and kick up Wild Irish Rose bottles from the dirt.

Those summers I would sit on my grandfather's porch, hunkered on the green wooden swing that hung from the ceiling, and watch them coming and going. Wordlessly, they labored up the brick sidewalk, bowed with the weight of their melons, past the flood marks my grandfather carved into the curb back in 1936. It was a mysterious harvest they bore, a harvest somehow urged from cinders, ballast, and river muck; I understood nothing of it. Unlike other boys in the neighborhood, I never tempted their wrath by raiding their gardens at night. I'd heard and desperately believed the tales of wild men who lived under the Panhandle Railroad Bridge, holed up like cougars in the hillside between the piers and the river bank.

Once one of those men stopped below the porch. Leaning over, he eased his load to the sidewalk, then wheezed up the first flight of steps. Pausing at the landing, he gazed up at me with a crazy grin on his face. His eyes rolled. The sweat stains on his shirt were brown with dust. Then, soundlessly, and with no warning, he dropped where he stood, snapping suddenly forward at the waist, like a broken tree. I shouted, astounded. He rolled over, lying on his back, arms out, eyes wide. A trickle of blood seeped down the planks from somewhere on the back of his head.

Though he'd only been drunk, and though, in fact, I watched him eventually regain his feet and struggle away up Logan Street, pursued by the diving hawks of abuse my grandmother loosed on him, I was convinced he'd died. What wove up the street and was lost in the elms and summer haze was a wraith, and I stood long over the smear of blood it had left as a sign on the landing.

Those summers were filled with such signs. At twelve or thirteen, a boy who spends his summers by the river becomes, in the mysterious transformations of self-consciousness and puberty, less a person and more a location, a pulsed setting, a living, shimmering place where riddles and omens take their most forceful life. He cannot ignore or deny them. He gathers them like shells, old turtle hooks, yellow scraps of iron, in the rough sack of his imagination. Late at night, in an upstairs room occasionally shaken by the passing of a mainline freight, the steam engine exploding silence into fragments that do not settle for a long time after, he lies awake and examines them over and over until they mix with his dreams and become a deep and secret part of him.

My grandfather, the god of that house by the river, whose late-night comings and goings in the midnight machinations of railroading only heightened the effect of his being on me, was one for signs and mysteries. His cronies were all legendary, minor deities with names like Hippy Allen and Hambone McCarthy, and they orbited him, as it seemed to me, like moons around some great planet. They told lies, endlessly, one after another, with the eloquence of preachers delivering sermons, Their prejudices—against blacks, against Italians, against West Virginians—were of the hardness of granite, and taught me, early on, certain sadnesses of America. But their language enriched my days with lusciously suggestive uncertainties: gandy dancers, the slab job, Brown's Island, shitepokes.

I sensed these men knew things, important things, and I listened when they gave each its name. When my grandfather took me fishing, to a secret place by the paper mill that he'd marked with a spill of tar on a rock, he'd tell me,"Watch for shitepokes, now. If they're flying upriver, you're going to catch a big one. But if they're flying downriver, all you'll catch is a cold." The handbook name for shitepoke is "little green heron." But no handbook I've ever read, then or since, explains the immediate, essential meaning of its existence for a man and a boy sitting beneath a cloud of willows, the fumes of Dill's Best pipe tobacco rising like an incense, katydids and grackles choiring in the brush.

Sometimes, we fished at night. The willows folded in against us, framing a lilac stretch of river that deepened, as the light faded, to indigo, then ebony, then disappeared. Only a brooding dampness remained then before us, tossed into ghost waves that smelled of catfish and silt when a tow groaned upstream. Catching fish in those nights was an exercise in faith. Blindly casting into darkness, testing the line for slack by feel, never seeing its slant into the water—all I had was the most filamentous, fragile connection with the river bottom thirty yards offshore, and with the lurking channel cat as long as my leg that I knew, that everyone in the neighborhood knew, lived there.

And when the first thrill of nibble tensed my hand and arms, and I gathered, slowly, my feet closer beneath me; when my grandfather fell utterly silent so that there was nothing of him beside me but the one red eye of his pipe's glow in the dark—then I was more alive, more frighteningly, excitingly alive than I'd ever been before. And when I felt at last the night fish's log-heavy tug, its slow but insistent drawing of my line, and then suddenly everything exploded as I whipped myself back and the pole came back with me, and I felt the hook set, and the pure heaviness I could struggle against—then I heard my grandfather's voice beside me, urging calm, urging patience, urging skill, and I knew I had all those things; I knew, now, something of the mysteries he and all those other men knew, and life was good, and deep, and rich.

The end of that part of the ritual came in renewed silence. After unhooking the catch, I washed my hands in the unseen river, hearing the stringered fish slap in muddy shore water, and I settled back to rest, and to savor again the smell of Dill's Best as it curled upwards through the willows to the stars.

After, the stories would come. One fish a night was enough. One fish a lifetime of nights was enough. Pap Pap would fill his pipe again, a match would flare, and his voice ride steady on the air. He told stories of the melon growers by the river. He told stories of drownings and rescues, and of the long sorrow of the Burning Lady, scorched in an explosion while filling a navigation light over in East Steubenville. He told the stories of Goodluck Scanlon and my great-grandfather Richard and of great-grandmother Madigan and bad luck and train wrecks and Money O'Brien, who was still alive.

Remembering all this, I have come to think that "growing up" is not the proper phrase to name the experience of those days. "Growing out" is more like it, or "growing broader." For those stories and those nights contributed little to my ability to deal with the mundane, practical realities of adult life. Rather, they afforded me a rich and always youthful, even romantic, lore. In many ways, I remain that boy, and am glad of it.

Because of that, I am often troubled by the reactions of people when I tell them I grew up in Steubenville. For as it is with races and religions, with accents and modes of dress, so it is with locales. They, too, can suffer the viciousness and ignorance of stereotypes. I have long wrestled with the fact that my hometown was, and is, an unfortunate place, a place where the monster of 19th Century industrialism flourished and then, as it eventually had to, floundered. The mills struggle, the railroads rust, the mines have fallen barren, creeks run ruined. Even my memory of a short stretch of work in the Steubenville Plant of Wheeling Steel is smeared with the town's dust and grime. I hired on in the Brick Department, and we stowed our lunch buckets under a bench across the mill from the open hearths. When lunchtime came around, we found to our dismay that a thin film of grit covered everything we'd packed. The stuff had even worked its way through the plastic wrappings of our sandwiches, and speckled the good Italian bread with shiny slivers of graphite.

But the insistence of that dirt, its universal coloring of everything in town—church fronts, sparrows, the standing water in ditches—is to me an emblem of the insistence of what was good about Steubenville, too. Like that inescapable dirt, my grandfather's stories, my summers by the river, my summers in the fields beyond the old strip mine above the house pervaded my boyhood, coloring all that I saw, all that I thought, all that I learned. A sediment of influences settled in me there, giving my life its foundation.

Being born—and that happening in one specific, one particular place—who can tell the mystery of it? Why here, and not there? Why now, and not then? Isn't this an omen, too, a sign?

I think it is. Turning the meanings of my birth and my birth-place over and over in my mind, as I turned the meanings of those omens and signs years ago in an upstairs bed by the river, I am reminded of Wendell Berry's words. "No life and no place is desti-tute," he writes. "All have possibilities of productivity and pleasure...that belong particularly to themselves." So I must not only labor to discover and, when necessary, defend these possibili-ties, but having found them, let them go, let them make their own meanings. To remember with only the facts is to fall prey to a kind of blindness. All lives, all places, must involve an element of fate and, more importantly, of myth, to be fully and vitally alive.

So, more and more, another, greater grandfather of those early days comes to mind. He lived alone, in a two-room house between the railroad and the river. His was the only place left standing in that no-man's land, and its walls were covered inside with the pic-tures of people I always thought I recognized, though he never told their names. His house was a relic, a reminder, a kind of sag-roofed shrine. Next to it, a buckeye grew, old and sparse, its top torn out by floods, drift and ice. But it spread valiantly, close to the ground, so close that its lowest branches were rubbed of their bark, the living wood touching the earth.

When the season came, that grandfather gathered the few dozen buckeyes in a pail, and laid them out along the house to dry. When they were ready, he passed them out to any boy or girl who passed on the way to fish or to hunt for river glass and stones.

"They're lucky buckeyes," he told us. "The eyes of them are keen. They watch out for you. And when bad luck's coming, they'll jump in your pocket to warn you. Smart people will pay atten-tion."

I still have mine. It's burnished with touching, shiny as a river-slickened stone, bright as the eyes of my grandfather telling a tale. It used to jump quite often, but it's been stiller, lately. I think it's telling me, "Remember. Don't deny, don't mourn. Remember. That's good luck."

And amid the cinders and railroad ballast, amid the omens and shitepokes and nightfish mixed in the inward soils of my remem-brance, I think something important has happened. I think that buckeye has taken root.

Basement

Our house in Steubenville, a 1950 vintage Ryan home, had no basement. It sat on a concrete slab smack in the middle of a narrow lot, modest, working-class, and with hardly enough headroom in its attic for the the ghost of a dwarf. It was a clean house with no mysteries, no thrilling staircases to tumble head-first down, no nooks and crannies to gather the debris of the years, no subterranean dampnesses breeding water bugs and mold. It even smelled new at first, and took several years to accumulate and ripen its own organic, individual scent. All houses have their own smell; once established, it is a permanence that lingers, dwelling like a secret under the masking fake florals of air fresheners and the bogus resins of pine-scented cleaners. It is the house's unique molecular signature, a complex mixture that blends the personal chemistry of its inhabitants with the esters and exhalations of its materials: plaster, caulk, moldings, lumber, plumbing. All of these, in turn, are compounded with the odors of the cuisine and even the pastimes of its occupants. One man who lived in my neighborhood refinished furniture as a hobby, and his house, redolent of tannic acid, smelled like an oak bog.

Children especially are aware of the odor of a place—I was, at least—and I think I might have been able to identify, even blindfolded, which of my relatives' or friends' houses I was in, simply by its smell. It is one of the special gifts of childhood, this acute sense, and I mourn the losing of it as much as anything from my youth.

My grandparents' house on Logan Street had its special smell. Their place was older than ours by a couple of generations, and its scent had matured in a time of coal furnaces, steam locomotives, and full-bore open hearths. These things it smelled of and more. When I stayed overnight there, I awoke each morning to the aroma of toast making in the broiler of grandma's gas stove. This was no run-of-the-mill toast. It was toast's zenith, the acme of bread. Beneath the alchemy of the open gas flame, those slices of Italian from DiCarlo's bakery were transformed, mixed with the varied compounds of that house's and that neighborhood's atmospheres; there has never been toast like that again. Its smell drew me from the upstairs front room, and its crusty, buttery crunch remains crisp in my memory even now.

My theory is that the proximity of the river had something to do with the quality of that toast, and with the taste and odor of the very days themselves there. Even in the clearest, most tangy weeks of late spring, the green darkness of the river two backyards away made vaguely musky the smell of the air. There existed a rich, silt-flavored micro-climate on lower Logan Street that even the buck-eye in the side yard seemed to sense, sprawling widely over the sloping lawn like a fat burgher having no need to get up and exert himself.

But despite the delights of the upper reaches of the house — the middle room upstairs, which had been my uncle Paul's, and where I first read *The Adventures of Huckleberry Finn* , and the old-fash-ioned bathroom with its claw-footed tub and black register hoods curved like the necks of gigantic cobras — it was the house's lower regions, even below the fragrant kitchen, that most drew me in those days. For my grandparents' house had a basement, a full deep one, and it came as close as any basement I've ever known to being the archetypal Dark Place. It was at once fascinating and frightening, a tinkerer's workshop and a Merlin's secret chamber, filled with vapors and dimness.

Its door opened off the dining room. The landing at the top of the stairs was an abbreviated one, crammed with cleaning gear and rummage, and it would have been more than an even bet that a child would trip there and fall down. Even grandma herself had stumbled there and broken her arm.

But there was an additional association that raised my consid-eration of the basement out of the domestic and into the realm of the mythic, even the grotesque. It came in the form of a tale that no one in my family remembers hearing. Perhaps it was one of my grandfather's private and arcane concoctions, let drop of a stormy summer evening on the front porch down there by the river. It could have been. Or maybe I dreamed it, years ago, lying abed just across the river from Fairy Glen, on whose dim, timbered slopes my father and I once discovered the body of a hanged man.

Whatever, I do not resist this story's substance now, nor did I then. It has entered me as places often enter me, entire, in excruci-ating detail, though seen only momentarily, perhaps, from the corner of my eye. The slant of light over a rockface, the webbed and shattering glint of a creek through a pine grove, the silhouette of a cottonwood snag far behind, glimpsed from the stern of a turning canoe — these scenes possess me, become moments that last, images that somehow re-shape the world for me.

So has this story, which I remember happening (maybe) long ago.

Next door to my grandparents' house, her fenced yard abutting the slope the buckeye grew on, there once had lived an old woman — call her Mrs. Rainey. She was a widow who rarely came outside. When she did, it was an event the neighbors noted. Soon it became apparent to those who caught sight of her that she was suffering from some terrible ailment. On her head she commonly wore a rag, wrapped turban-like around her skull at the level of her eyebrows. Over the course of a summer, the neighbors saw that there was a kind of growth, or tumor, jutting from the top of her forehead and causing the rag to assume a bizarre, horn-like shape above her brow. This growth swelled and swelled until it was the size of a large turnip.

The women of the neighborhood were appalled. They tried to get her attention, to communicate their concern; they sent a doctor to see her, but she refused to come out from behind her half-closed door. Week by week the growth under the headrag enlarged, and the women's dread deepened to despair.

And then, one hot August afternoon, Mrs. Rainey appeared in her backyard, spryly attending her stunned hollyhocks. The headrag was tight over her brow — it fit exactly — the growth was gone.

"I was walking down to the cellar," Mrs. Rainey told someone later. "And I wasn't watching close. I bumped my head, right there where that thing was. I squashed it up against the low ceiling of the stairs, and that thing busted off, fell right in my hand. Oh, it was messy, wet with watery stuff. Well. I cleaned myself off, and I wrapped it in some old papers. Then I put it out with the trash."

Standing at the forbidden landing at the top of my grandparents' basement stairs, gazing up at the cobwebbed ceiling, I imagined Mrs. Rainey, and, before grandma caught me and pulled me into the chandelier-blazed dining room, I thought I saw, in the dimness above me, a dark stain. It was peril and hope, disaster and luck. Even now, Mrs. Rainey's story continues to dwell in some limbo of my knowing, neither science nor religion, perhaps not even a "fact," but something stranger, more close to me than any of those, more chilling and more true.

Soon, I grew old enough to go to the basement on my own, gripping the banister, putting the old woman's horror out of mind as best I could. The steps leading down were wooden and the dampness had weakened them so that they gave underfoot, sagging beneath even the small boy I was. At the bottom, a black hulk looming in darkness, stood Pap Pap's guncase, a high varnished cabinet with glass doors. Inside it, he kept two shotguns, a World War I rifle, and his fishing tackle; the smell of steel and gun oil washed from it whenever it was opened. On the wall opposite stood his work bench, an eight-foot construction of two-by-fours and plywood. Piled high on it in the back against the foundation were old biscuit tins with perfectly fitting lids embossed with Uneeda or Nabisco, and amazingly stout little cheese boxes with dadoed joints. Above, hung from the joists by their nailed lids, gleamed twenty or thirty jars of screws and washers, nuts and bolts, hinges and angle irons, casters, connectors, tiny turnbuckles, and a hundred other to-me-nameless amazements of copper and brass and iron. All had been assiduously drenched with WD-40 to keep the rust off, and so the smell of oil dominated both sides of the basement. To a railroader like my grandfather—and an Irish Catholic to boot—rust was an avatar of the devil. The oil can was his holy weapon, a kind of exorcist's aspergillum.

It was at this same bench too, with its single light bulb overhead and the tiny window level with the brick sidewalk outside, that Pap Pap sharpened his knives; I remember the rhythm and silken friction of that sound: *shrop, shrop, shrop, shrop*, and I remember how the blades came from the whetstones gray and moist, and how, as he wiped them clean on his pants leg, they appeared wonderfully glinting and bright as he lay them on the bench, side by side, like slivers of razored moon.

To the left of the workbench was the coal cellar, in terms of domestic spaces now an extinct species. Too bad: the cellar and its cargo supplied an extra dimension of earthiness to the basement, and delivery days were a wonder. Delightfully frightened, I watched the great black chunks roar down the coalman's chute, and I held my hands over my ears to keep from going deaf. The cellar filled steadily, the coal pile creeping toward the door, dust billowing out into the basement. Tiny flecks of anthracite glinted in the light from the workbench window. Sneezing, I retreated to the clearer air near the bottom of the stairs, and the dust began to settle at once, a thin film on the floor. Then, slamming the little steel door, the coal man would be finished. I'd run upstairs and hang over the edge of the front porch to see him drive crazily away, his truck itself a thundering confusion of rattling fenders, clashing gears, and grimy blind headlights.

Cellars within basements, darknesses within dimnesses, illuminated here and there with startling lights—like a lived-in Chinese box, my grandparents' house contained spectacle within spectacle. For opposite the coal cellar, just beyond the gun cabinet, was the fruit cellar, another night place, another set of amazements. Its door had no knob, but a carved wooden handle, slick with forty years of nervous sweat and pulling. Beyond it a frayed twine hung in the center of its darkness, a ghost string, pale and forever damp. When I pulled it, the cellar blazed suddenly before me, astonishing and garish as a sideshow. Dozens of jars of preserves lined the wooden shelves: rich raspberry-colored beets, golden peach halves, yellow innumerable nuggets of corn, the frenched greens of string beans pressing the insides of their jars to bursting. But none of their summery garden smells came through. I was aware only of the cool alien mustiness of the cellar, of the decay and bitterness of its sour earth floor, of the rotting wood, the rafters shaggy with mold and cobwebs, and of the formic smells of dead insects—crickets, water bugs, roaches, the shiny black beetles with pincers like the horns of a stag. When I'd selected a jar of pears and clutched its coldness uncomfortably to me, I pulled the light string again; darkness swarmed up around me, and I instantly forgot all the bright fruits, the shimmering vegetables. The place closed in on me, smotheringly, and I fled, giddy with fear, into the gray light of the basement as if into the noon sun. I fastened the door behind me, pulled it shut deliberately, listening for the wooden latch to click, as if to keep locked inside it some horrid wildness. It was a wildness I already suspected lived inside me, in the cellar of myself, a place I could never completely escape, and so had to learn to live with. For consciousness was arising in those days, consciousness of the wonders of light and half-light, and as well an awareness of the strangely fertile but sometimes dangerous broodings of dark. No one could have kept me from that knowledge; no one could have—nor should have—sheltered me from its power. It was as inevitable as growth, that knowledge of the dual faces of the world, and as risky, as rewarding.

It is a telling coincidence, then, that to get anywhere in my boyhood required going down; from the ridge we lived on to town was a descent of several hundred feet down a winding hill road my cousins from flattest Missouri were afraid of when they visited; from town to my grandparents' house was a descent almost clear to the river; and so their basement was only the logical continuation of the shape and direction my life's journeys had already begun to take. As a boy, I dug a trench and a deep hole in our backyard, covered it with some old siding from a barn, and piled earth a foot deep atop it. I sat hunkered in that darkness lit by a single piece of candle and was thrilled. During my late adolescence, in pursuit of an education, I drifted a couple of hundred miles downriver, to Cincinnati, that many more feet closer to sea level, that many more millions of years deeper in geologic time. Now, as a man, I dig down each spring and fall in my garden, turning the soil, bringing the richness—death and life combined—up for another season of growth.

And I spend time in the basement of the house we live in now, and see, among my own recent and soul-less tools, the pleasantly haunted hand-me-downs from my grandfather: his oil cans, all filled by his own hand twenty years ago, his huge pipe-wrenches, relics of his steam-engineering days. I see his tool boxes, one red, one green, like the signals of his oft-cussed but beloved railroad, still decorated with the jig-sawed letters that spell his name. I meet him in the Dark Place through these things, these old familiars, these pass keys to the house we all share. It is a reunion in silence and shadow and the earthen smells of old time.

For the basement is to me, somehow, though on a larger scale, the equivalent to that pit, "one cubit's length along and wide," that Circe instructed Odysseus to dig at the end of his journey to the Land of the Dead. After the wanderer made his sacrifices, the spirits arose, and that pit was their meeting-place, the borderland between past and present, life and death. So the basement, too, is a border, an opening midway between the lighted, busy, careering world above it, and the ancient, secret, brooding earth around and beneath it. Standing here, I am exactly at eye level with the living, root-twined surface of the earth, yet my feet are as deep as the bottom of a grave.

But it is not the end of the journey, no more than Odysseus's visit was the end of his. Both up and down exist here, both past and present, and together, they may suggest the shape that is called future. I remember, when fear or sorrow begin, how old Mrs. Rainey, that miraculous day, was going down to the Dark Place. And I re-member — deliberately remind myself to remember — that she came up from it, out into the light, and that she was well.

Aunt Aggie

In her prime, Aunt Aggie had fished shad with her husband Earl from a johnboat they'd built from the wreckage of the last Wheeling packet. Around 1920, the *Esmerelda* had run aground on a bar in Cable's Eddy, just upstream of Steubenville. The pilot, an Irishman, had poured on the steam so hard the boilers exploded, blowing him and the rest aboard into pieces "so small," Aunt Aggie was fond of recalling, "you could have got five or six in a shotglass and still had drinking room."

We'd learned this from Aunt Aggie herself; no one else in the family, except for my older brother Jack, considered the subject fit for conversation. To my mother and father, those two were shantyboat Irish, white-trash kin to be forgotten. Their lives had seemed crazy and desperate in comparison with the monotonous business-as-usual routine my family always engaged in.

But Jack and I hungered for Aunt Aggie's yarns. We looked forward to those days when, liberating her for an afternoon from the nursing home, we would ride her around town in Jack's Ford, listening to her memories and tales.

"Up around Shippingport one time," Aunt Aggie began one summer Friday morning, after Jack and I had lifted her into the front seat, "Earl got in with this crowd of Guineas who were always on the lookout for easy money. One day this fella showed up with a box of dynamite, and got your uncle all excited about blowing up the river at Steubenville and selling the fish it would kill down at Mingo. There used to be a market there—folks came from all around to buy carp and bullheads from gunny-sacks full that people had to sell. Now Earl wasn't so thrifty he didn't need an extra dollar or two sometimes. Your father never trusted him for that reason. 'Get a white man's job,' he'd say. 'Get off this shady scheming.' But Earl, he'd gone along.

"What happened nobody knows for sure. But I expect that one of the men, maybe Earl himself—he couldn't go five minutes without smoking—lit a match, and the boat jumped up a wave, and the match dropped in among the dynamite..."

Aunt Aggie paused, looked dreamy and wistful. Jack and I kept quiet, trying to picture Uncle Earl. To us, aside from Aunt Aggie's stories and the creature our own imaginations had made of him, he was little more than a smudged face in a musty photo album our mother kept secreted away in an upstairs bureau, along with the rest of the ragged and flood-stained papers from that side of the family.

"And you know, I never cried," Aunt Aggie said. "I never shed a tear till that gal came calling a week after the funeral. She came up to the back door — this was down at the place on Benton Street — and she says, 'Miz Shannon, I'se the one whose skift was blowed up on the river.' That was Earl and his crowd all over — instead of using their own boat, they'd borrowed the first one they could find, from this black gal in the Bottoms.

"Well, I could tell right off she was dirt-poor, and didn't want to do what she had to do. But I let her in, and we sat at the kitchen table and had some wine and I wound up giving her ten dollars and crying like a lost child in her arms."

I tried to imagine Aunt Aggie crying like that, but it was hard. Though wasted and diminished now, like a piece of oak driftwood that's been a long time washed and scoured in the river, she'd been stout and well-fleshed in her day. And I knew, too, her spirit had been just as stout. It had been a trouble to the family all these years. Underneath their relentless anger, there had always lingered a sliver of envy in their curt, disparaging references to those days. The adults all seemed to harbor an excess of bitterness against them when Jack or I asked. Each time "that woman and her husband" — they wouldn't even speak Earl's name — were mentioned, faces grew flushed and my father would leap from the table, a mixture of frustration, disdain, and incomprehension in his voice, and pace up and down the living room, waving his arms, cursing those "damn black Irish." The only other times such emotions boiled over were when Jack and I committed one of those obscure boyhood crimes that my father could never quite name for us, nor explain the sternness of his punishment for.

So Jack and I had been attracted to Aunt Aggie and Uncle Earl at an early age. To us, they seemed our closest kin — rebellious, unconventional, wild, and similarly liable to our parents' strange rages.

Aunt Aggie fell silent after her initial burst of memories. Jack drove down North Fourth toward Flat Iron Park. Every one of the old houses along the way, we knew, was the setting for one or another of her stories.We'd often used driving by there as a way of getting her to talk when she seemed weary or withdrawn.

But the day was gray, and the flood of words about Earl had left her drained. When we passed the park, she hardly stirred. Her knobby hands, tan with the sheen of age, sunk deep in her hollow lap and only gripped themselves the tighter.

We drove up Franklin Avenue, then out North Seventh, past the High Shaft Coal Mine and the steep gob piles that smoldered behind the tipple. Then Jack swerved, at the last minute, onto upper Market Street, and the sudden motion jarred Aunt Aggie out of her silence.

She brightened as we climbed the hill past the abandoned brewery caves whose entrances had been cemented up to keep people like us from getting lost in them. There, Aunt Aggie had told us once, Earl himself had wandered for two days, finally escaping through a hole no bigger than a peach basket in the hillside down Cemetery Hollow, nearly two miles away.

Suddenly, she pulled at Jack's arm and said, "In here."

Jack waited for the downhill traffic to clear, then turned into the graveled area in front of the high retaining wall set against the rock of the hillside. From it a clear and steady stream of spring water poured into an ancient stone trough. This was where the horses of the brewery wagons had stopped for rest and water in the old days. Aunt Aggie sat relaxed, enjoying the sound, while Jack and I smoked. After a time, Aunt Aggie said, "It makes me thirsty, that water music." She turned as far around in the front seat as her stiffness would allow, and winked at me.

Jack looked at Aunt Aggie, then back at me, nervously. I grinned.

"Oh no," he said. "No sir. You saw what happened the last time. No way."

Aunt Aggie cackled, and rubbed her bony hands together with a dry rasping. "Oh, I'm thirsty, Jackie," she crooned. My brother went red at the collar.

Two weeks before, we had, for the first time, given in to Aunt Aggie's thirst—of all of her vices, the most legendary and therefore most heinous one. But all that afternoon, we had sat in the car on Benton Street, listening as she let flow a steady stream of reminiscence, pausing only to sip from the bottle that Jack occasionally passed her. She'd told us of the floods she and Earl had lived through, and at one point made Jack and me get out to walk along the stone curb until we found the notch she and Earl had cut to mark the high water line in 1936. By the time we'd gotten her back to the nursing home, she'd been bleary-eyed and stumbling. The doctor on duty had called our father on the spot.

Jack rubbed his thigh anxiously. "I'm telling you. Dad would kill us for certain."

"Stuff!" Aunt Aggie snorted.

She was fully recovered from her sorrow now. The drive up-hill, away from the smoke and dust of town, always seemed to lift her spiritually as well as bodily. She had a powerful capacity for snapping back from the weight of her memory's burdens; it was the gift that had carried her into her seventies with only minor and short-lived interruptions of zest. And drink, the ache for drink, was a part of her power: Aunt Aggie was thirsty, had always been thirsty; her thirst was linked to her largeness of soul.

Jack had no heart to deny her. He shrugged his shoulders and backed the car out onto the hill. At the top was a neighborhood grocery stocked with canned goods, cold cuts, and cheap liquor. When he stopped and got out, Aunt Aggie called after him. "Get that brandy stuff this time!" Then she settled back into the seat with her hands folded, content to look out the window at the shacks that lined the road, and to hum a few bars of a tune in a voice as brittle as tinder.

Jack got back in. "All right. Where to this time?"

Aunt Aggie smiled at him, and closed her fingers over the neck of the bag as tightly as she could. There came over her face a soft-ness we'd not often seen.

"Let's go down to the river," she said, almost in a whisper. "Let's drink a few with Earl."

The gray weather broke as Jack bumped the car across the Pennsylvania tracks and turned south on Water Street. Sunshine blazed against the crumbling red brick of the Pot House. All the dwellings on the river side of the street had been torn down years ago, victims of high water, neglect, and the forces of the lives that had filled them in the days when Steubenville was Little Chicago, wide open. Although the street had known Mafia capos and pimps, assassins and madmen spoiled by steel, or coal, or booze, it had also known a few innocents like Uncle Earl, greenhorn entrepeneurs with an eye for the quickest way out of that place.

But now, it was deserted. The upriver breeze swirled ghosts of clay dust from the Pot House up and down the shattered walks. In the heat, glimmering sloughs, flashing with shoals of shad, seemed to flood the hazy reaches of the street.

Aunt Aggie made it known she wanted out, to sit a while by the river. Jack and I lifted her from the car, her legs spindly and weightless, her fleshless, hard-ribbed back bowed as the hull of a skiff, and helped her over the curb. She shuffled slowly down the gentle slope to within a few feet of the shore. I went back to the car and brought the liquor and the folding camp stool from the trunk.

"Sit down, boys," Aunt Aggie said when I returned. "Sit down on either side of me, and keep that bottle moving."

That's just what we did. Jack and I sat down, one upstream and one downstream of Aunt Aggie, and she, perched high and erect on the stool between us, looked out over the river and sipped brandy, and together we were quiet a long time.

Memories began to move in me, memories or imaginings, though they were all equally vivid and brilliantly lit, and of the same warmth as my blood. I saw Aunt Aggie, young, face flushed, balancing in the bow of a johnboat as a man with a mustache and dark eyes hauled in a net from the stern. There were bank swallows skimming the water around them, skimming and circling, diving and rising. The water was smooth and clear and deep. Beyond the boat, on the West Virginia shore, a black man squatted on a river rock by his cane pole, lighting his pipe. The smoke was blue and large, and lingered in the still air over his head. Behind him, far above in the steep and riverward woods, a crow was calling, steady and regular, so that the sound floated out across the water. Aunt Aggie grew still in the boat, then turned her eyes away from the man in the stern to the sound of the crow in the woods. And when she turned towards the stern again, there was a patch of light, a brilliance of air and nothing else, nothing forever to talk to and laugh with and fish with and drink with again.

And when all that faded, I began to sweat. The liquor rose in my head and heated me there. I found myself dabbing at my brow.

There was a dark spot across the river, a grove or thicket, low on the banks, that my eyes kept returning to. The spot had something to do with Uncle Earl. I did not know how I knew, but I did. It was directly across from me, exactly opposite the Pot House. Consciously, I would pull my eyes away from it, and gaze far upstream at a daymark in a stand of willows across from the foot of

Benton Street, then down again, past that dark spot, to the piers of the bridge where I could see the head of a barge tied off to some trees just around the bend. But always my eyes would return to the dark spot, and when they did, a bead of sweat would roll into them, and they would burn and blur.

And then I was conscious of Aunt Aggie, shifting her stool, moving her feet. And when I looked up at her, she was gazing steadily at me, pale and stricken, her red eyes rimmed with tears.

When we got back to the nursing home, Aunt Aggie was woozy. No one there was sure, but they all looked hard at Jack and me as we walked her to her room. Then the nurse, a stingy, angular woman who smelled of disinfectant, helped us get her into bed and squeaked off, frowning and wordless, down the dingy hallway.

Jack looked at me helplessly. Aunt Aggie smiled up at us, gripping our hands weakly. After a time, she drifted off to sleep. I laid her hands straight at her sides, smoothed the blankets, and we walked out of the room.

At the entrance desk, gunmetal gray tainting his strained face, stood father. When he saw us, his face tightened even more. Jack murmured, "Hell. It's coming." The frowning nurse glanced quickly over her shoulder as she fled down a corridor.

Father said nothing. Glaring, he motioned us to follow, and we trudged out into the parking lot. He got into his car, Jack and I in the Ford. Though the sun still shone, gloom drifted in all around us. We drove slowly through town, letting our eyes fall where they would, on the shabby storefronts, the dusty streetlamps, the broken men on the corners.

When we sneaked in the back door at home, Mother was sitting at the kitchen table, a cup of coffee before her. She did not look up as we passed.

Father went to Jack's room first. The voices were loud, Jack's apologetic at the beginning, but steadily more defiant. I could hear my father, exploding with righteous authority, claiming common sense. A silence followed. Then the door, slamming, shook the house.

I waited. I could hear Jack banging things next door. Then I rose from my bed and went upstairs to the room with the dusty bureau. I opened the album to the smudged face of the man with the mustache and dark eyes. Then I closed it, carefully, and came back to my room. I paused at the door, then went in. At my desk, I took out a piece of cardboard, a pencil, and a sheet of cut-out letters for stenciling. I pressed hard so the outlines would be clear, then filled the letters in. I opened the door, peeled the old letters off it, letters that spelled "Patrick" — a stranger's name, a child's, a name I would not sign nor swear by nor answer to again. And I put up the new name, the four fine letters, the capital E boldly black, and I stood back and smiled with Aunt Aggie and Uncle Earl and the peace that glowed inside me. Then I slammed the door as hard as I could, daring those people downstairs, those people with thinned and fearful blood, to try to shout the three of us down.

Heaven, 1957

Solemn High Mass at the Easter Vigil. I'm nine and I'm standing at the very edge of the choir loft of St. Peter's Church in Steubenville, the oldest parish in town, staunchly Irish Catholic since its beginning before the Civil War. And this is pre-Vatican II Catholicism, and before me, up on a stand so high that if she fell backward, she would plunge sixty feet to the floor of the Church below (but even to think that she could fall is simply impossible — God does not allow such things) — high up before me, then, Sister Malachy directs the men's, women's and children's choir of one hundred voices, and I am chanting, solo, the Litany of Saints, and the whole choir is responding:

Santa Lucia, *orate pro nobis*
Sanctus Michael, *orate pro nobis.*

And the air is filled with incense and song and light, and I am trembling with fear and pride, a soloist at nine, with my parents and my Pap Pap and my grandma and all my cousins and aunties and uncles down below, and the cassock and surplice I am wearing are heavy and starched and smell strange and white and holy like the hands of the nuns who washed and ironed them in the convent just across the playground by the church and Mrs. Gilligan, the organist, is in a kind of ecstatic state, her eyes rolling back in her head as she hits the great Alleluia chords, and all the men in the choir with their deep voices — men who drive beer trucks, men who work in the mill, men who fix cars — they too are in cassocks and surplices washed by the sisters, and maybe they too, as boys, had the same sisters teaching them the lives of the saints in school, but now tonight their polished shaven faces are flushed and gleaming with sweat — my God, I think, they're all angels — we're all, for the hour and a half of Mass — we're all angels, and heaven is right here, in the light and smoke and song of the choir loft, Sister Malachy levitating, almost bodilessly rising before us as if on the swells of the song, and she is coaxing out of us the great Hebrew Hosannas, the beautiful Greek Kyries, and all this — the Greek and Latin, the incense and organ tones that get you deep in your chest, even lower, that resound in your groin, and make you want to melt into it, give in and be taken up by it, to circle the dim shadows of the dome overhead, the stained glass glinting from the candles below, but the dark night pressing all against them from the outside, and the incense gathering to a nimbus up there, and the strange dream I have of kneeling there, on the tiny ledge around the bottom of the dome, all alone, on a red velvet kneeler, and that is somehow heaven, not pleasant exactly, but holy and high up there and alone, and Sister Malachy now floats three feet above the platform, and all the choir men's eyes are closed, and they are lifting her up into the air on their voices, grooms accompanying the bride she is as she meets her husband who is God and we will get to see him, we will be there when the great burst of light appears with the Alleluia and Amen and Monsignor Grigsby below will explode into a thousand candles, *orate pro nobis*, and Sister Malachy and Sister Mary Anthony and Sister Mary Hubert, *orate pro nobis*, will turn into white birds, and the music will be clouds to walk on, *orate pro nobis*, and it will be heaven, right here, the mills all gone, the dirty streets all gone, the mill dust rubbed off the stones of the church revealing gold and more gold, and it is heaven, *orate pro nobis*, heaven, Sister Malachy, heaven, Mrs. Gilligan, *orate, o kyrie kyrie kyrie eleison.*

Small Bright Things, And Flash, And Glint And Glitter

By the time I was twelve or thirteen, it became obvious that I needed glasses. After several years of mediocre learning, during which I had fallen into the habit of squeezing the corner of my eyes to wedge the grammar lesson into focus, I was bundled off to the eye doctor. He was a dazzlingly pink bald man who smelled of Listerine and whose chrome gizmos and lens-snapping contraptions made me giddy. I squinted and mumbled in his darkened chamber, and it was done. Within a week, a pair of Buddy Holly Specials with frames the color of used crankcase oil appeared on my desk. Just beyond them stood the warm blur of my mother. "Try them on," she suggested. "No," I said.

There is nothing so fragile as the ego of a skinny and pre-pubescent boy. This is especially true if he attends an Irish Catholic grade school that boasts a winning football team, a school song ("The Wearing Of The Green") brought stateside by ruddy tenors who belonged to the IRA, and at least one future NFL athlete. I was surrounded by brawny boys and bonny lasses, and so was even more acutely aware of my scrawny frame, my big ears, my skinhead haircut—even my stupid shoes. The last thing I needed was to wear glasses.

Had I known of such things then, I would have cursed my own DNA for conspiring against me. To be fair to history, though, had I been able to see past my own nose, I would have recognized that physcial eccentricities, like wacky eyesight, for example, were a distinctive feature in my family, like the noses of European aristocrats, or the extra fingers of certain royal clans. They set us apart. My own mother's ears stick out, and my Pap Pap's were prodigious, with long wide lobes that hung inordinately low along the lines of his jaws.

But back then, I was desperate. I refused to wear those glasses. This lasted a year or so. I accomplished such a lengthy disobedience through a simple ruse. I'd wear my glasses at breakfast each morning, but as soon as I got out of the house, headed for the bus stop, I'd whip them off like Clark Kent ducking into a phone booth and jam them in my pocket. For the two most beautiful girls in the city would be on that bus every morning. They were high school girls, a thousand years older and wiser than me, but because their names rolled melodious and golden and in my dreams—Margie and LaDonna Chilenski—I felt it important that they view me as something more than a nerd, a foppish tyke in galoshes and goggles.

It all collapsed one afternoon late in the sixth grade. My father showed up at school and delivered a duplicate pair of glasses. It was an obvious ultimatum. Sister Mary Ursula called me to the office—in itself a huge embarrasment, a setback which was the source of nightmares for years—and there stood dad, the old thunderheads roiling about his temples. I returned to class like a felon stripped naked save for his grotesque and klutzy spectacles. I blushed my way back to my seat. Out of the corner of my eye, I thought I saw, in my hallucinating grief, Bridget Boylan, the great beauty, razz and gape at me. My life as a stud was over before it ever began.

But I could see! Wasn't it strange and interesting how Sister Huberta's wimple cut so cleanly against the black of her veil? Wasn't it a wonder how the wainscoting on the outside of the cloakroom was so beautifully grained? Wasn't it touching the way Linda Kirkpatrick's patent leather shoes gleamed so sharply in the light that poured over the oiled window sill?

Bespectacled constantly, I marveled. The world had changed, suddenly, completely. The corners and edges of things grew sharp and defined; objects in the distance were no longer blots of mysterious color and movement, but real Buicks and towboats and cops. Up until then, I had lived in an Impressionist's world: there is no more immediately accurate way of describing the iterations of color, the layerings of texture, the indefinite visual buzz and hum of things as I saw them without glasses. Trees with their edges off more or less evanesced into the atmosphere around them; I could see no sure demarcation. Objects blended with one another like the dabbed patches of color on an artist's palette. There was a charge, a kind of electrical aura to leaves, branches, clouds, the scales of snakes; they shimmered and sparked and were resonant in the slightest breeze, the most subtle shift of light. Heisenberg's Uncertainty Principle was alive and well in the lab of my own treacherous eyes.

All of which may seem to have been a handicap. For I was not seeing the world truly, but through the distortions of my flawed eyes. In a sense, my vision was a handicap, but as it is with such things, I learned unconsciously to compensate. For example, I became adept at reading, from a distance, the language of walking. I could recognize the gait of a friend half a block away, though I could not make out clearly what he wore. Roger Swartz had a curious double-clutch in his step; the heel came up, paused, then carried through. This created a kind of bounce in his walking, and it was this, as well as the way his shoulders moved and his trunk leaned against the air, that I could recognize long before the features of his face set off the memory cell that stored his image in my brain.

Similarly, since I was interested in birds, I had to learn their characteristic flight habits or their songs in order to identify them at a distance. That small something aloft at the edge of the woods near the strip mine: a goldfinch, surely, for its flight was a merry undulation of sprint-and-dip, sprint-and-dip, attended by the tinkling of small brass bells.

I compensated in grosser, more technological ways as well. For some strange reason, my father kept his binoculars — good 7x 50's with a wide field — stashed between the undershirts in his dresser. When there was something down the street I wanted to see, I'd rush in and grab them, then sprint back outside and stand in the middle of the road holding them up to my face. This looked as stupid as it sounds, and one day it became clear to me that I couldn't go through life with Bausch and Lombs strapped to my face. It would be hell on my love life, for example.

Actually, my poor vision turned out to be a productive disability. For much of my childhood, those years when the world is still fresh, its unspoiled novelty as vibrant as the spots on a channel cat, I lived the life of the microscope. I came literally face-to-face with astonishments people with better vision overlooked.

I was walking in the woods one afternoon. I had hunkered down to look at something on the path before me, then glanced up and to my right. An elm stump had sprouted there, the tallest shoot four or five feet tall. And there, on the underside of one of its leaves, motionless, clung the most beautiful beetle I'd ever seen. I still remember its scientific name: *Calasoma scrutator*, The Caterpillar Hunter. It is a wonderful insect with an iridescent green carapace edged with a line of brilliant red, and it is one of the largest beetles in eastern Ohio. I had probably walked past hidden dozens of them in my life, yet it was my need to get close to the ground to see that resulted in this first discovery. The beetle's beauty, its wild and secret life carried on a few yards off an old lane in the woods, someone's radio playing in a garage just behind the trees—all of this caused a kind of mental shift that I could almost physically feel. It was as if the world had suddenly snapped into focus.

Another afternoon, I was clambering down a bulldozed slope at the edge of a new housing development in the neighborhood. Smashed trees and huge slabs of sandstone had been pushed into a gully; ten yards further the woods started, a good woods, big beeches and maples and hickories. Near the bottom of the gully, an undisturbed log lay flanked with weeds. Leaning down, I saw a familiar caterpillar on a leaf, stretched out to its full length, but oddly still. I looked closer. At even intervals about a sixteenth of an inch apart and down both sides of its back, there were perfectly round holes. The thing was dead, hollow as a straw. I stepped back, frightened. But I looked again, and I was sure. Later, after I had carefully removed the leaf the husk had dried to and carried them home, I read about the parasitic wasp that lays its eggs on the skin of such caterpillars. When they hatch, the larvae, maybe two dozen of them, burrow in and feast slowly on the living worm, gradually digesting its organs and tissues and displacing them with their own fattening bodies.

It was better than the Saturday matinee horror movies my uncle Paul had begun taking me to in those days: better, and more real, and so more genuinely chilling. And it was all the result of not seeing well far-off, of the necessary hunt for small bright things, for flash and glint and glitter: tiger beetles on the sand of riverbanks, craneflies wild in a clearing by the creek, the dazzle of an indigo bunting at the edge of a field. Close-up, those things were more my world than the hills that blocked the horizon all around Steubenville. Long before my father showed up at St. Peter's School with my glasses, the real had been formed for me, and it was a reality with an illumination and brilliance I still miss. Even now, if I want to see something close-up, I take off my glasses. And when I do, I become young again, and the world blurs and rainbows far off, while the object I hold in my hand becomes the center of everything, my only possible focus. Magnified, its colors more deep and more rich than they ever are when I wear my glasses, the creek stone or cicada or beetle is all. I have come to understand much better that line in Walt Whitman's "A Noiseless Patient Spider," the line in which the soul, "seeking the spheres to connect them" in his great metaphor for seeing and knowing, is at once "surrounded, detached, in measureless oceans of space." Surrounded by the great blur and hum of the ocean of sight as I was in my boyhood, I was at the same time, in those moments of looking, "detached." And what I saw in that focused and intense detachment was a world of detail, richness and intricacy.

Perhaps I am drawn to dwell on all this so much because I now have two boys of my own, and their training in looking and seeing — their apprenticeship to concentration and awareness of the small things in the world — is in my hands. The chore is doubly difficult, not only because I must somehow help them learn to resist, in Edwin Muir's words, "the vast dissemination of secondary objects that isolate us from the natural world," but also because they both have quite good eyes. They will want to look beyond the horizon — and this is good. But it is not good if in looking beyond, they fail to see what is right in front of them, close-up, on the ground at their feet. I would be doing them a disservice to allow them to grow up strangers to the wonders of their own place and liable to the false allurements of the manufactured world's superficial flash. One sowbug in the backyard, really looked at, really seen in all its jointed, intricate, amazing texture and detail, is worth any thousands of cheap gum-ball prizes. Knowing that animal, earth-colored, hugging the ground, its life a mystery to unfold, is the true and real astonishment, the finer, more worthy adventure.

Menagerie

In the spring of 1959 or 1960 the alligator arrived. It came in a nondescript cardboard box a little longer than it was wide, of just a size to contain a tiny umbrella or a couple dozen pencils. But the shipping label said Florida, and when I lifted the box, a scuffling hiss issued from it that sounded promising. My mother stood in the doorway of my room and shook her head. Some friends of hers, hearing that I was interested in animals, had sent the thing along. I had noticed, over the past year or so, that my mother's interest in animals was waning.

Earlier that spring, I had come home from school to find her sitting at the kitchen table. "Hi, mom, " I said.

"Hello," she answered wearily. "Your lizard is on the back of the chair in the living room. Please get it back in its bowl."

That had been an eastern fence swift, a handsome animal with steely scales and a deep blue swatch along its back and side, and gifted, as its name indicates, with great speed. It was difficult to catch when it squeezed out of the cheap glass turtle bowl of the kind they used to sell at Woolworth's and McCrory's. I'd put a piece of old window screen across the top, but the more tenacious or clever creatures frequently escaped. Now mom looked winded, and a bit peeved, and I hurried to get the swift back into my room.

And there had been the run-in with Mr. Peterson, the man who hauled our trash. During warm weather, I kept snakes, sometimes as many as half a dozen, in the shed my father built in our backyard. Mr. Peterson found serpents objectionable. He explained as how he'd have to stop hauling our trash if they remained; my mother made me drape tarps over the fronts of their cages on collection day, so that Mr. Peterson could at least imagine they were gone.

There had been others too: the rabbit called Penny that lived for a while in a hutch along the shed, several generations of doomed McCrory's painted turtles, schools of fancy guppies which reverted over unselected generations to their original drab and minute forms, box turtles, dogs, parakeets, various insects in both adult and larval forms, and a lethargy of anoles, skinny displaced creatures which the dimestores sold as "chameleons."

But it was the alligator that finally exhausted my mother's indulgence. Actually, it wasn't an alligator; it was merely cousin to an alligator, a spectacled cayman to be exact, and it was about a foot long, and as mean a beast as I'd ever tried to keep, with the exception, maybe, of a knot of queen snakes that used to give me bad dreams with their nasty attitudes and pink mouths.

I don't know why, but I expected a certain docility from the animals I kept. Goodness knows I was aware of their instinctive wildness, which I admired, even when it unsettled me. I remember watching a bizarre occurrence once from the back of a friend's father's pickup truck. A cicada flew down to the ground and crawled into a small hole in a claybank by the road. A few seconds later, a great wasp, almost two inches long, with a wingspread of four, and as garish in its markings and color as the dazzle camouflage I'd come to know from building models of British warplanes, landed at the entrance of this tunnel and crawled gingerly in. It was a cicada killer, and its usual living was made by stinging its prey with a paralyzing agent stored in abdominal glands, then lugging the motionless victim by main force high into a tree. From there, the wasp would clutch unto its breast the stiff cargo and glide back to its burrow in the ground, all the while losing altitude because of the cicada's great weight. Having safely cached the still-living insect in its burrow, the wasp would then lay an egg on it. Later the larva would feed at its leisure until at some critical point of devouring the victim would give up the ghost and the wasp larva promptly pupate and metamorphose into an adult next to the husk of its former roommate and meal.

My friend and I both knew these facts by the age of nine, as we did other startling and bloody histories of the animal and insect world. Thus we watched agog this suicidal and unnatural drama. We even talked his father into digging into the bank with an old entrenching tool he kept behind the seat, and we found, yes indeed, the expected tableau: wasp and cicada, the one fresh egg already laid on it, jutting from its abdomen like a tiny white knife. Why had it flown to sure destruction, actually seeking out the deadly wasp's lair? What deal had been struck, up in some buzzing tree, between predator and prey?

Mysteries, prodigies, anomalies: for children only haphazardly self-trained in the rudiments of Life Science, still mythic and animistic in our understandings of the world and its phenomena, these things piled up around us, making of nature a kind of great squirming, protean riddle, something like one of those misleadingly simple drawings in which are hidden (and you are challenged to find) a penguin, a whale, a zebra, an ostrich, a porcupine, a lemming, and a blimp.

And why shouldn't the world of plants and animals be prodigious and mysterious, packed with turbulent wonders? The world of the mills in which many of our fathers worked was just such a place, though cast not of flesh and breath but of metal and fire. There, the blast furnaces roared like the most terrible of dinosaurs, and above them the skies glowed with a ruddy vitality. To enter the mill (the gates were always there, standing open but guarded, always guarded) was like entering an underworld, and the stories that issued from the Slab Yard and the Open Hearth and the railroad sidings were as awe-inspiring to us boys as the sagas of Boone and Crockett, Scott and Amundsen, Stanley and Livinstone.

Another time, down from our neighborhood, we were digging in the hillside at the source of a tiny spring that fed the creek. A great wet log sat directly over where the water seeped from the ground, and as we tried to clear the way, it crumbled in our hands. There, amidst the red decay, glowed a brilliant salamander, bright yellow with dark crimson spots. We took it home and put it in an aquarium and then looked it up in our *Golden Book of Reptiles and Amphibians,* by, I think, Frank S. Zim. And there it was: a western spotted newt. It was always exciting to find an animal or insect in our books, but this was doubly so. Consulting the map that accompanied its description, we saw that the range of the creature we had in the basement aquarium extended no further east than the Mississippi River. We had lucked on to a newt that should not have been found within four hundred miles of Steubenville.

Had we been scientists, we might have taken it to a zoo in Pittsburgh, or to the little Nature Center at Oglebay Park in Wheeling, and had it all explicated and made clear. But we were pagan, innocent of orthodoxy. We were boys, and dreamers, and we squared ourselves to this anomaly as to any other. Nature was unpredictable and mysterious, and often it was *our* secret. The western newt was for our eyes and ears only, not for grown-ups, not even for other boys: just for us. Nature singled us out for instruction now and then, and if the lesson was unlikely, we were not surprised. Unschooled in laws and probabilities, we expected to be left wondering. "'Tis strange," Horatio says of the ghost on the midnight battlements of Elsinore. In our expectant ignorance, we were as accepting as Hamlet: "Therefore as strangers let us give it welcome." We had no other choice.

It was that very strangeness of the world, I think, that attracted us to it. Its otherness, its unwillingess to speak our human language, and yet its apparent attempts nevertheless to communicate itself to us, as in the case of the newt, kept us close and attentive.

For several years of my boyhood I crawled through the woods at the top of the hill, inspecting the big coffee cans I'd buried to their rims below the underbrush. I'd read that these pit-traps were particularly effective in collecting beetles. For me, the most beautiful and varied tongue Nature spoke was Beetle. Had I known it then, I would certainly have affirmed J. S. Haldane's claim that "nature has an inordinate fondness for beetles."

I especially liked the grammar of beetle life. It encompassed practically every ecological niche from parasite to predator, water to mountain-top to air; in size the beetle was fluent from the microscopic to the the monstrous: the Goliath beetle, one of my favorites, six to seven inches long, was relatively easy for collectors to find because in flight, I'd read somewhere, "it sounded like a small plane." Beetle was also the most geographically dispersed of nature's languages; the family was a kind of zoological Esperanto, spoken on alp and in rain forest, on ocean beach and desert dune, and studying it seemed to link my local study with the world. It was a way of being global, this beetling, even when I worked in a closet lab at home.

From those cans buried in the woods I plucked out dozens of obsidian-black scarabs of several species, cordovan-colored staghorns, and the teardrop-shaped bombardier beetles that emitted a puff of gas that exploded with a tiny pop as they fled. Their varieties and shapes, their secret existences literally under our noses, meant something as I pondered their forms and habits, as I recited their names over and over, as I learned the intricate Latin and Greek of their study. Coleoptera, the scientific name of their family, means "sheath-winged" and to me it was of huge interest the way beetles had to spread those chitinous sheaths first, before they could unfurl their wings and fly: as if a convertible had to lower its top before it could start its engine. *Plastron, dorsal and ventral, papillae, carapace, thorax* — even the vocabulary of beetle study was itself a part of the secret we shared.

But more than all this language and knowledge and sense of connectedness came from my working among nature and the beetles: I got a sense that there were alternatives, other ways of being and living, and though I do not think I articulated this sense of diversity to myself as a child, I still think it helped shape my view of life.

Within earshot of the mills (you could hear the hiss of the blast furnace being tapped regularly, every day and every night, everywhere in Steubenville) you might be hunkered over a handful of beetles in the woods, far down Beatty Hollow, rapt in the unlikely gingerbread of a foreleg's architecture, and then abruptly become conscious of the mill. There was, you remembered, a whole human furnace of activity and transformation going on in another world, a world you realized that though within hearing physically was really farther from the beetle's world than the most distant galaxy was from your bedroom.

And so one of the things nature spoke to us was this: in the very moment that you become aware of your distance from the beetle, and the mill from yourself, the very moment your consciousness wraps around those large facts, you realize how alone you are, how utterly alone, how strange and alien. It is as if the sandstone bedrock of your neighborhood suddenly splits and shifts, and forever after, you are never able to stand in the same place your were in just a second before.

With all of the animals I kept, I was trying to gather unto me, hospitably (how sinister the connotations of *hospital* in that word), fellow neighbors, and to learn something of their world. But theirs was inhuman and distant, unfathomably distant. I worked hard, trying diligently to create a habitat exactly like the one the animal had come from, whether it was the western spotted newt, or the common Alleghany salamanders that we collected from under rocks in the creek, or the beautiful black snakes we'd find in the brush along the strip mine. I'd dig up the soil from where a mouse had been, and all the moss and lichens, and I'd feed it whatever I thought it had eaten in the wild, and I'd watch it, closely, for whatever it had to tell me.

What went through my head as I spied on those things? Was I expecting them to behave naturally, as if they did not sense that they were out of their element and on display? How little I knew of the relationship of the observer and the observed in those days.

Perhaps I thought I could vanish; perhaps I thought that through some effort of spirit and will I could stand so still, so silently, that I would become mere background, just another part of the landscape, and so see the behavior of the snake or turtle or shrew just as the mountain saw it, or the moon, or the boblink flying overhead.

No chance: the hum of human consciousness is the original sin; its background noise on the planet is now as ubiquitous and as audible as the background hiss of the Big Bang throughout the universe. I am never so loud to myself as when I am trying to be quiet; I can only suppose this is equally true about me to the fox or deer or wild turkey nearby.

Whitman's escape to the non-human is no answer, either. "I think I could turn and live with animals,/ they are so placid and self-contained..."

No, I don't think I could. I have already tried that, living almost ferally in the woods for months at a time, and I have seen that it doesn't work. I can no more survive in the snake's lair than it can survive in my scrubbed and vacuumed bedroom. So almost always, like single bees in jars, things died on me. I discovered, in grief and frustration, the inseparable connection of living creatures and their place. My desire to have them where I wanted them, where they were convenient to my whim and idle curiosity, but isolated from their own environment, was fatal to them in every single case.

The root of "menagerie" is in *menage* —"of the household or family." What I learned was that the human family and the human household did not include nor provide comfort and shelter to, the wilderness, be it in the form of a woodland plot of ground or the snake that glided over it. "Menagerie" can only make sense in exactly the opposite of its root meaning: a menagerie cannot be a household of pets torn from their actual habitat, but must always be a part of the wilderness, the Earth Household, as Gary Snyder puts it.

The alligator died, under my bed, among the lint and dust and lost pennies of the human household. Its body had grown light as balsa wood, its belly shrunken, its formerly large moist eyes dessicated, blank and dull as split peas. It had been instinctively hunting for Florida, and shallow warm water, and live food, and instead it came up against plastic baseboard. The household had been too small, too isolated from the intricacy that life requires; the arrangement failed.

I buried it outside, behind the shed, in the compost pile, where it joined grapefruit rinds, eggs shells, and coffee grounds and went back to a sweet obliviousness in the mix and slow smolder of decay. There was, finally, a kind of chemical joy in its last identifiable days as alligator remains, but I believe I was the only one conscious of it. The principals involved, those elementary butlers and maids, those builders and enablers and dismantlers of life, didn't even know there was a party.

The Snake Man

When I was ten or eleven, the notion entered me to look for snakes. I had seen snakes before then, of course, but these sightings were accidental, unplanned: walking back through the woods on the way to Fox's Den or Sunshine Cave, I'd freeze in my tracks as a blacksnake appeared on the path before me, a glinting swiftness that dissolved in the shadows and light as soon as I had seen it, uncertain as a dream. Mostly, I'd doubt my own eyes, convinced that it had been only a shifting illusion, but then I'd find a length of shed skin between two rocks, and I'd pick it up and look at the sky through its scaled transparency, and wonder.

So I decided to firm things up a bit, to actually search out snakes, see them in their own places, and be convinced. I did not have to go far. Up the street from our house was a hillside lot, bulldozed out of the sandstone and shale, with a number of great flat rocks lying about. My friend and I chose one, hoisted it, and there, glory be, lay a snake. It was an Eastern Ring-Necked, a slim beauty of slate gray with a pale yellow ring just behind its head. Eighteen inches long, it lay in a loose S in a depression under the rock, and it did not flee. I nabbed it between my thumb and first two fingers, and it coiled calmly around my wrist like a cool bracelet, weightless almost as my skin. I took it home and kept it in a jar while my father and I built a cage from an old dynamite box and some porch screen. The snake lived, apparently content, in the cool shed all that summer until I turned it loose when school began.

A few weeks before that, a friend of my father's, Dutch Riesling, visited us. "I hear you got you a snake," he said. We walked back to the shed and I showed him the Ring-Necked, and he allowed as how it was a fine specimen, and rare. "Your Ring-Necked is a shy one." he said. "Don't hardly ever see such, they're so quiet and secret."

We stared into the cage a while longer, and as we were about to leave, he reached up to his chest. "Course there's some snakes that ain't so small and dainty." With that, he pulled a three-foot pilot blacksnake out of his shirt, and I stood agape as it wound itself tight around his arms, coiling almost clear to his shoulder. It was a fine animal, sleek and dry, with a dark moist tongue that fluttered like a puff of smoke from its mouth, and with steady calm eyes and perfect round pupils, black as India ink. Dutch let me hold it, and I felt its heft, its actual muscled weight. Any lingering doubt I might have had about the reality of snakes was therewith dispelled. That blacksnake occupied actual space and time; I could feel its powerful vitality clenching on my arm.

Often after that, Dutch and my father and I would go on hikes, looking for snakes in the summer, or for fossils in the winter. One December, up on College Heights, we stood next to some huge boulders that had been torn out of the land by bulldozers clearing the place for the new university. The rocks were full of brachiopods, shiny gray fossils the size of a thumbnail or larger, their fan-shaped shells piled one atop the other, and millions of years old. Dutch chipped one out, whole, and lay it in the palm of my hand. "That there animal has come a long way to get to you," he said. "You think on that hard, now."

In all the chances I had, in all the possibilities of men I could have met and been influenced by, it was two or three that luck would have me cross paths with as a boy. Forrest Buchanan was one. He was the namesake of the Forrest Audubon Club in Steubenville, and I still remember the talk he gave to the members one autumn evening in 1957. Pythons swallowed pigs, and brilliant hand-sized morpho butterflies floated through the Amazon forest he described—still the primeval one, forty and more years ago, not the ravaged staggering giant it is now, with bulldozers and roadbuilding machines scavenging its ruined wilds. I sat in the front row, amid the ladies in their hats and the gentlemen in their coats and ties, and decided that I, too, would go to the Amazon, dare to wade its piranha-infested rivers, breathe in that same incredible humid air, see all those jeweled wood-boring beetles. And I'd write it all down, and save it.

Mike Swartz was another. The father of my best friend, he hunted coons and collected helgrammites in the riffles of creeks, monsters we had not known even existed. Once, driving back from one of those trips, Mike had stopped in the road to pick up a blacksnake, a big one, and it had wrapped half of itself around his forearm and the other half around the seat frame of his truck. He'd had to drive back leaning wildly to his right, unable to shift gears, and his son

Roger and I sat in the back of the truck, trembling.

And there was Dutch. He worked on the Bell Telephone line gang with my father, and had been a scout master for years. His easy familiarity with snakes, and his outgoing, laughing manner made him a favorite guest speaker in elementary school science classes, where he'd often pull off his snake-in-the-shirt trick. A serious outdoorsman, he camped every summer in the boondocks of Canada with his wife and boys. He was a welder, too, and along the walls of his garage workshop stood tanks of oxygen and actylene, and sometimes when we'd visit he'd be working out there, crouched like a witch doctor in a shower of sparks. In the center of the garage for a season or two stood a 30-gallon galvanzied garbage can, covered with a square of coarse hardware cloth weighted down with a brick. At the bottom of it, motionless, smelling vaguely of cucumbers, lurked a 30-inch copperhead.

Dutch was an old-timer, hand-building things and repairing them himself, still knowledgeable and enthusiastic about what many would call "the old ways." He knew the names of plants and birds, insects and trees. He knew, first hand, the ways of the weather, and the slope of land, and the suggestion of water a line of sycamores, seen from far off, made. He knew how to build a fire in the rain, and how to sleep comfortably on the ground. A native of a town scarred by industry, its skies ruddied by the glow and smoke of the mills, its creeks yellow with acid run-off from old mines, its hills stripped and barren, he nevertheless walked with his senses clear and his mind on Nature.

He probably has little idea of how much he and Forrest Buchanan and Mike Swartz and my father affected me, or how they made me aware of the other, secret lives — of titmice and nuthatches, of Ring-Necked snakes and katydids — that were carried on with a strange and exciting intensity just beneath the urban veneer of my place. Though a part of the working world, accepting the necessity to labor for others at a job, he never lost his ability to live really in his awareness of Nature and wildness. He held what seemed to me his most secret strength in reserve not for mere work, but for life. For him, that meant much more than the daily routine of the domesticated, urban human. For him, that meant keeping snakes, literally and figuratively, close to his heart.

Remembering Dutch and his reptiles, I am reminded that the world is not only a human place, but a place of a thousand thousand other kinds of beings, voiceless, unlettered, but whose acquaintance is an occasion of growth and delight, even a deep kind of wisdom. Most of the life on this planet lives under a rock, or beneath the surface of the sea, in a burrow or crevice, or aloft in a windblown tree. I might have sleepwalked through life, if it hadn't been for Dutch and the others. I might have made the common mistake of thinking and living as if buying was always better than listening, that progress meant growing more and more deaf to the voices of the forest or pond, that a microwave was always better than a campfire, that a roof was superior to the stars on a cloudless night, or that the best thing to happen between myself and a snake was distance.

Carp, And Other Lessons

It was in the fullness of summer, a fervid August day in my boyhood, and Charley Joyce and my brother Dennis and I were fishing for carp at the foot of Logan Street in Steubenville, near where the gas line crossed the river just above a sewer that chummed with garbage the carps' very kitchen.

This was before girls, puberty, self-consciousness — in the unblemished open innocence of youth. We had two pounds of fresh anise-flavored doughball my grandfather had made, and we had a whole day before us, and the river was green and the bank swallows fat with flies and the little Vs their beaks made as they skimmed the water widened and widened, opening like all possibility.

And my God, we caught fish. For two hours, there was no period longer than five minutes when one or another of us did not have a fish on the line. It was a frenzy of fishing, an outburst, an exclamation. Eventually our home-made stringers filled, and we piled the bodies of the carp around us on the shore, bunkers of flesh still slowly heaving and bowing in air, the coarse scales glinting, the gills opening and closing silently, sucking shadow and heat.

We buried our carp in the garden for fertilizer in those days; we did not eat them. Black people ate carp, white people did not. I never questioned this distinction; I simply noted and obeyed it. White boys could sell their carp to the black people on Dock or Benton Street, but nobody white ever ate carp, nor even spoke of eating carp, except to say they never would. Later, as teenagers, we laughed at the old joke recipe: take a carp, nail to a two-foot board, cook over fire. When crisp and done, throw away the fish and eat the board.

We did not think of eating carp that day. Charley and my brother and I simply hauled the fish in, twenty, maybe thirty of them, fifty or a hundred pounds of them, until we'd used up all the doughball. Then, reluctantly, we went home. I do not remember what we did when my grandmother saw us with them, though

I imagine we grinned and blushed with pride. I do not even remember if my grandfather saw them.

But in catching them, we entered history, walked through its
scarred portals, and there mingled with legend and myth. Every
fish story we'd ever heard, however unlikely it had appeared at
the time, however stretched and embroidered, became undoubted
gospel in those lucky hours, and would remain so the rest of our
lives. America's mythic abundance became a part of our personal
experience. Yes, we could say, there are fish in that river. Yes,
there are hundreds, thousands of fish. Yes, some of them are so
big they break your line. Yes, they are beautiful, even though they
are carp, and yes, some of them are even goldfish, orange and
heavy as pumpkins when you haul them up the bank, and they
don't fade so much, even when they die, as the green-gold mud-
dier ones.

When I was an even smaller boy, maybe in 1954 or 1955, walking with my grandfather on the Pennsylvania tracks, I remember
seeing from afar three tiny black children dragging a carp across
the rails. It was so large that they heaved and jerked at it as if
dragging a sack of coal. Still, the thing hung up in the ties, and
one of the kids had to hunker down and lift the tail end up and
over. Even my grandfather was impressed; he stood watching,
shaking his head, until the kids and the fish were out of sight.

Such carp compelled my imagination as a boy, as did the
sightings of giant catfish, the rumors of paddlefish and lunker
flatheads. And there were the soft-shelled turtles that Mr.
Schaeffer, who lived behind St. Peter's school, occasionally kept
in huge washtubs on his back porch. The turtles nearly filled these
tubs, two and half, three feet across, and in their strange smooth
shells were often lodged the deformed remains of .22 bullets wise
guys had shot at them from the banks. After keeping them for a
few days in clean water to purify their flesh, Mr. Schaeffer would
kill them and make turtle soup.

We ate catfish from the river frequently. They were mostly
bullheads and what we called yellow cats, and they averaged a
pound or two, and though Grandma Hague fried them nicely in
cornmeal, they still tasted of mud and oil. Once in a while, there
would be a channel cat, bigger and sweeter tasting, and I kept the
heads of the largest ones, their mouths propped open with wooden
matches, in jars of alcohol in the shed behind our house as a kind
of informal Museum of the Catfish.

But we never ate carp. The official word was that they were so full of bones they were dangerous, if not impossible, to eat. That couldn't be: we knew well that black people ate them. Besides, every year, all the children from St. Peter's trooped over to the church, and we knelt at the altar rail as Monsignor Grigsby pressed two fragrant beeswax candles against our throats and blessed us in the name of St. Blaise as a charm against choking. Much later I learned that the Chinese, those geniuses of the edible, ate carp. To prepare them they simply ground the whole fish up, bones and all, and fried balls of the stuff in oil and ate them with relish. But there were no Chinese people on Logan or Benton Street, so the cultural indoctrination that taught me carp were undesirable remained parochial in the worst sense.

It was a class issue and a race issue, and I did not know it at the time. Former aliens themselves, brought to America about the same time as the great 19th century European immigrations commenced, carp stood for such divisions; they incarnated the pockets of fear and bad custom and superstition and ignorance in the country. The reason we did not eat carp was not because they had too many bones; the reason was not that they were bottom feeders, scavengers, and thus unwholesome (catfish feed off the bottom, too, after all.) No: we did not eat carp because black people, and especially poor black people, did. Mustard or collard greens? No. Black-eyed peas? No. Chitterlings? No. But stuffed grape leaves? Why yes, that's another story. Gnocchi and pasta i fagioli? Sure, that's another story. Kielbasa and piroshkis? Most certainly, that's another story: white people's food.

I don't know how systematically this rule was promulgated, but it is clear that it was an unwritten law inherited, without question, from the previous generation. Slowly, I became aware of other rules like this.

For example, whether you liked it or not, football was good and manly, and whether you believed it or not, football was important. How did we learn this? How was it taught? Certainly, to make such distinctions and judgments could not be presented officially as the school curriculum in Steubenville; nevertheless, the lessons got learned.

Football, in my mind at least, was somehow connected to the mills. We were thirty-five miles from Pittsburgh, the home of the Steelers, and I remember one dusty August afternoon in a stadium next to the mills in Weirton, West Virginia, watching Bob Ferguson, the rookie from Ohio State. Touted as the back who, in all his years as a Buckeye for Woody Hayes, had never been thrown for a loss, he went down behind the line of scrimmage on three consecutive plays in that exhibition. It was easy to figure out—after all, he was up against the mills, and the men of the mills, the Steelers: you couldn't run against industry. It was bigger and tougher than you. What was good for Weirton-Pittsburgh Steel was good for America. You either ran with it, or you lost. For Weirton and Steubenville and Pittsburgh and Follansbee and Ambridge and Carnegie and East Liverpool and all the other company towns up and down the Steel Valley, industry meant life and jobs and schools and success and money, and football was connected to those things.

We played compulsively, addictively, when we were kids. Before my first organized football season in the eighth grade at St. Peter's, I had played for years on a ragtag pickup team made of almost all the able-bodied kids in my neighborhood. We played our games on a field scraped from the edge of an abandoned strip mine. Turf was out of the question: what you hit when tackled was slate, hard as a blackboard, or clay hardpan as unforgiving as concrete. Once, at the bottom of an on-going pile-up, I lay screaming as the weight on my ankle grew and grew until I felt it snap. I hobbled back home, a quarter of a mile, on that broken bone, my ankle swelling so severely that they had to cut my engineer boot off. Within a week of two of the cast's removal, I was trying to play again.

I remember another time when I had deeply bruised the muscles in both my thighs. Rather than resting, I kept on playing until at last I couldn't even walk. Not long after that, in a pick-up game against a bunch of boys from my high school's freshman team, I separated a shoulder. My father, a former high school player himself, a rangy center and fullback, though always concerned about my well-being, was fit to be tied. Finally, his patience and sympathy worn out, he blustered in exasperation, "Come home with another broken bone, I'll let you pay the doctor's bill!"

But the greatest game each year was the grudge match against the Dairy Bar Gang, a bunch of feral punks who lived in the hollow along Sinclair Avenue, down the hill from our ridge. Wells Creek flowed there, yellow with run-off from the strip mines, and the houses were small and built tight against the steep hillsides. Half a mile up this hollow stood a ramshackle neighborhood store, sided with the cheap tarpaper that some white people called "nigger brick." Every afternoon and evening kids hung out there, yelling at people who passed in cars or pitching pennies against the Dairy Bar's crumbling front stoop. In the summer, some of them terrorized the black children who tried to swim at the public pool nearby. The first time I ever saw the beating of a black by a white was when one of the leaders of the gang pummeled a child at Beatty Park. I looked on from far down the pool, in the moment before the lifeguards stopped it, as if frozen. It was clearly an attack; it was clearly racial; it was clearly another episode of the bullying those hoods had come to engage in with impunity.

And it worked. All that summer, and the next, no blacks swam at Beatty Park. If you were white, and someone wanted to insult you, he would tell you to go swim at the CRC—the Central Recreation Center, the public, unofficially segregated pool for black children, down on Washington Street. Where Beatty Park was a place of shade and century-old trees, clean and well-maintained, the CRC was a poor sister, surrounded by concrete and crowded. It was back to the CRC that the punks had beaten the black children. The message had been clear.

This is not to suggest that our game against the Dairy Bar Gang was to avenge our black brothers and sisters, or to show any kind of solidarity with them. Far from it. We simply didn't know what— or how—to think of such issues. We had no training for it. So we were fighting our own fights, the ones we did know about: the Dairy Bar Gang were hoods, they wore DA haircuts, a few of them even sported knife-scarred leather jackets. The stories of their back-alley rumbles were recounted on the school buses, and most of us boys from the hill had suffered an attack, with one of them on one of us, always a smaller one of us, covering up, defending, and a larger one of them, fighting dirty.

So our revenge was personal and mean, not ideological and altruistic. We wanted to get them on the football field, where knives and kicks to the groin were not a part of the action (honor among thieves?—so too honor among street-wise hooligans and bums— football had its rules, after all), and where we knew we could, to put it deliciously and bluntly, kick their sorry asses.

Which we did. And the satisfaction I feel even now as I write this is, I think, the greatest indictment against the rule of football over our lives. Conspiracy, the legalizing of revenge, the blessings of town and culture on outrageous competitiveness—all of this was no less a threat to our development than were the unwritten rules of racial segregation. I don't want to beat this too hard: I enjoyed football, and played it with an amateur's abandon, but there were better things I could have done.

Still, in the one year of official team football I played, what agonies and defeats! At ninety-three pounds, I played tight end. St. Peter's was in a league of all the Catholic schools in town big enough to field a team: St. Peter's, the Irish kids, St. Stanislaus, the Polish kids, St. Anthony's—two of them—one from Follansbee, West Virginia and one from Steubenville, both made of mostly Italian kids, and then the more ethnically mixed Holy Name, and Holy Rosary from the middle-class west end of Steubenville, and St. Agnes, from Mingo Junction, another mill and railroad town just a mile down the river. It was a 120-pound limit league, but there were always kids who were a little bigger, and they made a difference, especially when they were running backs.

As a tight end, I made one great catch and one great run, and upon them I build, however unsteadily, my entire claim to understanding the deepest agendas of the sport. The catch was in a game against the St. Agnes team. It was a quick slant over the middle; I had to leap high to catch it; I was hit by what felt like a train in mid-air; I watched with interest as my own cleats revolved above me in slow motion against the reddish glow of the Mingo Junction sky, and I remember nothing after that except that I held on to the ball. This was decades before high-fives and spikes and other demonstrations; if any of us had dared to show any emotion, our coaches, Scooter Dugan and Paper Abramowicz, would have looked at us as if we were two-headed calves. My greatest satisfaction was that when I returned to the huddle I still had all of my teeth.

The run was an end-around, and it was against St. Stanislaus in a scrimmage at North End field, a dusty sink squeezed in between the neighborhood and the railroad at the foot of the old Panhandle Bridge into West Virginia. I took the handoff and ran like hell, and there was only one guy in front of me, the biggest kid on St. Stanislaus—I don't remember whether it was Mieczkowski or Kuzikowski—and I just put my shoulder down and ran right into him—and over him! Oh Lord, I had broken into the clear and I ran and ran, and vaguely, distantly behind me I heard a whistle blowing, and guys yelling, and after another twenty steps I stopped (there were no chalk lines to mark the end zone) and I looked back and saw all the St. Stanislaus guys spread across the field, and the coaches and my team all laughing. I had run clear past the end of the field, broken away, passed beyond. And as I trotted back, I relived in my thrilled flesh the crashing into my opponent, and his falling aside, and the rush of power in it. And I realized that the rush was as dangerous a thing as I'd ever felt except panic in my life, and I began to shy away from it, right there at the very moment of the experience, as one shies immediately away from a fire after being burnt. From that point, there on the dusty North End field, after a touchdown in a scrimmage, began my decline as a player. Though I continued to play football often and hard throughout my boyhood, that instinctive wariness of its power made of my play a kind of counterfeit, a sham.

But I did, after all, continue to compete: I had to. That was the rule. Boys in Steubenville played football, and if they didn't—well, it was almost unthinkable. What the hell *did* you do, if you didn't play football?

I realize that this may sound crotchety and judgmental, smacking of sour grapes and calling into question all the lives and educations accomplished by boys who played football in Steubenville and won athletic scholarships. There were kids from the very teams I played with and against at St. Peter's, like Danny Abramowicz, whose father played with my dad in high school and who I've already mentioned was one of our coaches. Danny went on to Xavier of Cincinnati and got a solid Jesuit education and then signed with the New Orleans Saints where he set team and league reception records. He coaches now with the Chicago Bears. And there was the Steubenville St. Anthony's player Jules DiFederico, recruited by Woody Hayes from my high school class, and, sadly, whose mother was killed by a car while walking to a game at Ohio Stadium. And there was Pat Madden, from St. Agnes in Mingo, an outstanding student and a key figure in the Yale-Harvard game of 1969. And Buster Yannon, who went to Nebraska a couple of years after Harry "Light Horse" Wilson of Steubenville's public high school, and challenged all the older player's records. There were dozens of other boys, too, including my buddy Tommy Ciancetta, who went on to play at smaller programs like the one at West Liberty State Teacher's College in West Virginia. Each of them has his own story to tell, his own explications of the football rule to conduct; this is just one, by a minor figure unqualified to stand even at the edge of the field, but who presumes to do so, nevertheless.

It is the late Sixties, and I am working as a fireman on the Penn Central railroad out of Weirton, West Virginia. On an afternoon in late August or early September, our engine idles at the entrance of the mill near the Slab Yard, where flatcars loaded with ruddy steel just off the rollers line up to cool.

Into the cab steps a huge fellow, dusty-faced and tanned: a brakeman. He starts yelling at the engineer, and what he yells is the story of his son's first scrimmage as a member of the Weirton High school football team. An offensive tackle, his son had apparently been beaten badly by his opposing number, and the brakeman's mingled curse, rebuke, and lament builds and builds. The engineer tries to calm him, but there, amid the sunlight's dusty slant, the sharp scent of hot steel, and the fume of diesel exhaust, the man begins to weep.

Five years earlier, in physical education class, sophomore year at Steubenville Catholic Central. The coach is measuring boys' biceps, waists, and thighs, preliminary to the first round of the Marine Corps Fitness tests. I step up and crook my arm, making a muscle. He smiles, looks up from his tape and says, "You look like you're pretty tough. Why aren't you playing football?"

I tell this first story because it suggests the extent of the rule of football over some peoples' lives. I tell the second, despite the first, in part to make amends for not playing football, at least for the organized high school team. I didn't live up to the rule, all said and done, and not all my tackles and runs in sandlot games, not all the triumphs over the Dairy Bar Gang, not even my letter in track and the broken arm I suffered in the pole vault pit in Mingo Junction could make up for it. In the idiocy of my regret, and as if a squirt like I was, never weighing more than 125 pounds at any time throughout high school, could have done anything of note on the football field, I still feel like I let someone down, still sometimes feel as if I missed something important.

The mills and the railroad are linked, literally, to the third of the major unwritten rules of my boyhood. For it was the mills and railroad that connected the two sides of the river, and there were many Buckeyes who regretted the lamentable accident of geography which placed West Virginia right next to Ohio. From my earliest memories of riding in a car, I recall the epithet "hoopy!" being shouted when some particularly aggravating piece of driving occurred ahead. I don't know how long it took me to figure it out, but at last I realized that a hoopy was a West Virginian, and that when one came across the Fort Steuben or Market Street bridge to Ohio, he seemed to lose all his driving skills (if he ever had any: Ohio people seemed to believe not) and did the stupidest things on the road.

Over time this rule, whose skewed logic went something like this—all West Virginians are hoopies, all hoopies are bad drivers, and all bad drivers are naturally inferior people—began to sink in. Later, working on the railroad in Weirton, I saw it reinforced, even if some of the crews were West Virginian. If somebody screwed up, the engineer might mutter, "goddamn hoopy" and look over at me with a scowl.

I know now that it wasn't about driving. It was about hillbillies.

We didn't use the word "hillbilly" around Steubenville, not to my knowledge, anyway. "Hoopy" served the purpose in our parts. I've only recently seen the word in print, in my friend Tim Russell's poem "In Consideratione Praemissorum," which appears in his collection *Adversaria*. Tim and I have talked about the word; he has several theories of its origin. My favorite is that it was a name for fellows who lived south of the Mason-Dixon line, fellows like those who made barrels in Wheeling, or more particularly, for those who forged the bands of iron that bound them together: the barrel hoops. Thus "hoopies." By extension, the word also means the region itself, as in Tim's poem, which begins with a number of men sitting on a railroad tie near the mill at the very moment their lunch break ends.

> There is vacancy in their eyes.
> They naturally think of home here,
> down home, downstate, down "hoopy,"
> where they return to hunt or just to touch
> the leaves of a familiar bush...

In daily life in Steubenville, though, the word was freighted with a clearly negative connotation: us Ohioans were naturally superior—in speech, dress, employment, cuisine, pastimes, and driving habits, to mention a few of the more important areas—to those hoopies from across the river.

And indeed, even television seemed to reinforce the stereotype. I remember watching the original news special on Appalachia, which aired around the time the country was declaring the

War on Poverty. The production crew had selected the most isolated and most ramshackle of dwellings in the darkest and most depressed and barren hollows they could fine, and by this, as my late friend Jim Wayne Miller might have said, America came to know the mountains.

Social and economic class again shaped our perceptions. I am sure that the high muckamucks of Weirton Steel, living in their new ranch homes on the developed ridges overlooking the town and the river, were not perceived as hillbillies, even if their roots went so deeply into the Panhandle that their great-grandfathers had been slave-holding Virginians. I am sure that the Italian yardmaster at Weirton Junction most certainly did not think of himself as a hillbilly. And yet all he or the CEO of the mill would have to do was to drive across the bridge, and if he so much as stopped short at a red light, or didn't signal a right-hand turn, the Ohio yahoos behind would honk and jeer and chalk another retard up to inbreeding and ringworm and bad food.

This kind of baggage I had to drag around for a long time through life. And even though I have tried consciously to jettison every bit of it, some still lingers, I am sure, in the niches of my attitudes and behavior. It's a test that life sets up, but doesn't really believe in, deep down. It lays these hidden agendas, these unwritten rules, these ways of behaving before us like suits of clothes, and it urges us to try them on. Once we have, finding how they strangle and choke, it then invites us to buy them on the installment plan. "No thanks," we say, and life moves on, looking for the next set of dupes to test.

I don't know. There are people I lived near to in Steubenville whose versions of the rules might have been so utterly different from mine as to be almost incomprehensible. Others may well have lived lives as powerful and tragic and heroic as any stories in world literature, but they have not been told. Often I have wished that I could spend some time with Mr. Peterson, the neighborhood trash man when I was a boy, and the only black person I spoke to in my boyhood more than in passing. He lived on a farm and actually killed and ate his own chickens and ducks. I am sure he would have bought all the carp we could catch. But I wouldn't ask him about that now: I would ask him what it was like to be black, in the Fifties and Sixties, in the Steubenville I didn't know. I would learn a whole history of my home place that has yet to be told.

Until I hear Mr. Peterson's story, until I hear the full story of the Coulters, a family of eight or nine persons who lived in a trailer up Paddy Mudd Road and who went to St. Peter's, I do not know my place. It is astonishing how little we know about one another's lives. Astonishing and shameful.

So any attempt to tell the story of one's life must needs leave so much out, because it is unknown, unimaginable, and perhaps forever irretrievable. It is, in significant part, how one's life looked from the outside — from the point of view of the Mr. Petersons and the Coulters and the Weirton brakeman's, and all the kids black and white, Midwestern and Appalachian, Polish and Irish, with whom and by whom that life was shaped. It is how it looked from the point of view of Life itself, and History, and these are such huge and ever-changing things that we can never achieve their lofty vantage point.

Down here in the crowded local, carp flying from the river like miracles, children weeping, hearts pumping, games a-playing, hates building, birds skimming the water in utter innocence, the truth is a matter of grace and diligence and a kind of trusting, imaginative guesswork. There were as many boyhoods in Steubenville as there were boys, but not all of them are recorded, put down on paper, where they might be examined at leisure and at length, revised and re-thought and even, to some extent, invented. Not to mention the lives of the girls and women there, the daughters and mothers and maiden aunts, the grandmothers and midwives and nuns whose stories are yet another thing entirely.

Once, past midnight, I held in my hands a great bronze-green carp. Its body, in the chill night air, was strangely warm, the same temperature as the river. In the glare of the flashlight my grandfather held, it shone beautifully: a fish of bronze and malachite, a fish of gold and jade, a treasure of fish, a hoard of living beauty. I wanted suddenly to know everything that fish knew, the darkness and depth of the river, the world-bits cargoed invisibly by, hour after hour, century after century. I wanted to know all that was meant by that fish's life, and why it lived in such secrecy and silence, so near and yet so far away from us living, working, eating and dying on the bank. And I swear it is as if all this happened just a moment ago: just a moment ago I lowered my hands into the river. Just a moment ago, that fish slipped back into mystery, and I let it.

To Live Like an Animal

"Get your butt kicked you cut school again," his father said over supper. "Boy fourteen ain't got no business with that. No business." He pointed his fork across the table, and the boy saw the glob of potatoes on its tip. He studied it closely.

"You do it again I'll make you wish you hadn't. You'll eat with the dog in the shed for a year. Don't get your schooling, you'll see what it is to live like an animal."

They ate in silence after that. His mother hunched in her place, leaning, it seemed to the boy, away from the white heat that still rose from his father next to her and filled the tiny kitchen. He was troubled by something the boy had never figured out. He would come home from the mill and sometimes its heat came home with him, smelling of slag and bitter chemicals. Most times, he was able to keep the heat inside him, but now and then with no warning it burst from him in sharp jets that seared whatever they touched.

His father stood up from the table. The boy stared at his plate until his father had walked into the living room. Then his mother stirred and in a soft voice said, "You can help with the dishes, Jacob."

He was relieved not to have to walk through the living room past his father right away. Doing the dishes now was good luck. He scraped the plates as his mother ran the water. He hoped she wouldn't ask him why he'd done it. "Only the second day of school," he could hear her saying. And in his mind he felt himself turning hard and silent and having to hurt her with his silence.

As they worked, though, she said nothing. He dried as she washed. After wiping each dish there was time for him to think before she finished rinsing the next. The brief stretches between dishes became busy and troublesome in his mind. He tried to calm himself by watching her hands, their paleness reddening gradually, dish by dish in the water, and the white suds sliding down her wrists as she lifted each one out.

But it didn't work. The wet skin and paleness and the scent of the detergent upset him.

"I'm sorry," he said, desperate to leave the whirl in his mind. "It won't happen again."

"I hope it doesn't, for your sake, Jacob," she said. That was all. Her voice was flat, emotionless, transparent as water.

When they finished, he stacked the bowls on the upper shelf over the sink where she couldn't reach without stretching. He noticed how small she had gotten in the last year, how much more yellow her hair was becoming, not silvery gold like he remembered. For a moment, as she put the butter in the refrigerator and paused, as if about to say something before she closed the door, he saw again that she was beautiful, and it startled him and saddened him to be reminded of that.

"Did they give you makeup work at school?" she asked as she turned to go into the living room.

"Yes," he lied. The suspension rules required zeros in every subject for the day, no makeup allowed.

"You'd better do it, then," she said, and there was the same flatness in her voice, the same careful holding back.

"Yes," he said. "I'll do it."

* * * * * * *

He sat at his desk, arms submerged in a yellow slough of light from the light. A notebook lay open before him, glowing white as a fogbank. Though the air in his room was close and warm, on the dark uncarpeted linoleum, his feet were cold.

He did what he most dreaded to do now, but which he knew, somehow, he had to do. He let go.

* * * * * * *

Healey stood before him on the high board. "One-and-a-half with a half twist. Watch."

Healey leaned back, hands gripping the rail, then rocked forward once, twice, and began his approach. Three steps, arms raising from his sides, then sharply down and up, both feet planted, knees giving then pushing off. The board rebounded twice as Healey rose, tucked, dropped his right shoulder, twisted and rolled, then reached for the water. The last Jacob saw of the dive were the bottoms of Healey's feet, perfectly together, toes pointed. The sound of his entry was clean, abrupt.

He waited until Healey climbed back up and stood on the top rung of the ladder. "She's watching," Healey said.

Stretching forward, both hands on the rail, Jacob glanced to the right, out beyond the chain link fence that surrounded the pool. Up in the concrete bleachers sat a girl in a bright green bathing suit, knees together, her long thin legs carefully to one side, her head angled toward him. Both her arms were raised, and she was drawing a comb through the brass-red gilt of her hair, hair so long it lapped the small of her back where she sat. She paused as Jacob's eyes met hers, then finished the smooth drawing of the comb through and rested her arms on her thighs. She did nothing but watch him then.

Jacob breathed in deeply. He could feel Healey behind him, waiting. He straightened, took the first step, and gave himself up to it.

* * * * * * *

His father sat with his back to the door in Father Hennegan's office, rough hands clutching the chair's arms. When Jacob walked in, the principal looked up, and there was a warning in his eyes, and pity.

"Come in," the priest said. "Let's talk about this."

It was the Thursday after Labor Day. High school—Jacob's first year—had begun on Tuesday, and he had skipped on Wednesday. Though the priest and his father asked him time after time, he would not tell them where he had been, nor what he had done. Instead, he heaved a silence up before him like a great stone, tightened himself, tucked in and hunkered behind it, waiting for them to grow weary.

It ended with his father growing angry, even the principal, his face ashen and stiff, shrinking from the heat of his words. His father paced the office, settling down only when the priest stood suddenly and said, "Well, Jacob understands the consequences. It's not a good start for him. But I think we've settled this from the school's point of view. Mr. Whetsel. Jacob. Good day."

His father smoldered on the way home. Jacob leaned against the car door, trying not to think. They drove through town, but here and there through the breaks in the trees and buildings, Jacob could see the river, spread like a slate sheet under the gray sky. He began to blink each time it appeared, but its image stayed under his eyelids in the dark there, a cold band of white that went red then yellow, fading, but never completely disappearing.

* * * * * *

"That's her?" Healey said when Jacob pointed her out to him one day in early summer. She stood by herself in the entrance to the girl's dressing room. She wore a brilliant green bathing suit and her hair glinted. "Damn," Healey whispered. "She's beautiful."

Her name was Annie Finn. She lived on Starr Ave., a street cut into the side of the hill that rose behind the pool and above the rest of the hollow that stretched narrowly half a mile back into the woods. He'd seen her first in June, right after school was out. His friends from Holy Name knew her, and one afternoon he'd spoken to her. Almost every day after that, they'd sat together on the stone wall leading up to the pool, not talking much, but enjoying being with one another.

She was different, strange: calm but vivid among the rowdies and hoods that came to the pool to test themselves against one another. He did not understand at all why she let him hold her hand, nor did he understand the thrill her voice bred in his body. He did not know exactly what happened inside him when, for a shy moment when she had turned away, he allowed himself to look frankly at her slim body that already, somehow, hinted at a ripeness whose scent and fullness he could hardly imagine. Had she been a bird or flower, he would not have known the name, but would have lingered under any circumstance to learn it. That she was a human being, a girl, and that she was beautiful and would hold hands with him—he did not understand how it could be. So he learned not to try, not to struggle to name it, but to let time go, and names, and to sit in the day beside her, quiet, complete.

* * * * * * *

Healey caught up with him as he was heading out the doors to the bus. It was the first day of school, and the rush and whirl of it had made him nauseated. The other knowledge he carried numbed and deafened him. He'd heard it on the bus that morning. When people who knew him—and knew her—looked up as he passed on his way to the back, they fell quiet and turned their eyes away. And so he had not been able to concentrate, losing his way in the halls, forgetting what his teachers had told the classes.

"Jake, did you hear?" Healey said. "Crosley told me at lunch. She was out in her uncle's boat, and they were running up the river, fast. They crossed behind one of them hydroplanes and jumped a big wave. Annie was sitting in the stern, and she flipped over backwards."

Healey had spoken in a breathless rush, but suddenly he stopped. Jacob gripped the door handle, kids rushing past, yelling, laughing.

"Shit, man, I'm sorry," Healey said, his voice weakening. "Crosley says the prop hit her. She went right under it. Her uncle cut the motor as soon as it happened. But he couldn't find her. He went nuts. He ran the boat around and around until he was out of gas. Then he dove in. Somebody had to drag him out of the water. He was crying when Crosley saw him about an hour later. He was crying and the police were talking to him and the boat was just jerked up on the bank below the guidewall."

Jacob nodded his head, looking from side to side.

"Yeah," he said. "I know, I heard."

"Look, Jake," Healey said. "They still haven't found her. They're dragging the river now. Crosley's uncle and his dad are helping."

"Yeah. All right," Jacob said. "Okay."

The bus was crazy with voices. He found a seat in the back, next to a window. When the bus lurched forward he grabbed the seat ahead of him and held on.

* * * * * * *

It was two miles to the river. School buses passed him all through town, and his satchel, weighted with books, made him list to one side and then the other until he dumped it as he crossed the tracks and labored across the riprap below the bridge to the path leading down the bank. The fog thickened the lower he went; soon he came to a willow clump that forced him out into the river, ankle deep, and his feet were wet then, and he shivered.

Below the foot of Dock Street, he began to hear the boats. He could not see them. Fog deepened, already a bad memory, and with it came the voices of the draggers, muffled, faint. He walked on, feet crushing glass shards and mussel shells, spooked grackles bursting up and out of the willows, gray frights in the close air, then gone. He scaled the fence of the Water Works, slipped over the intakes, and slowed.

A wrecked barge loomed, its bulk buried in sand, only its rusty bow careening up through the clay and rubble of the bank. He sat down, leaning against it, and listened.

He sat that way an hour. The sun was burning the fog off gradually, and with the increasing light came the sounds of more boats. Their motors droned as they moved slowly up the river, then back down, then up again. At the end of each pass, he could hear the sound of chains clinking the grappling hooks, and suddenly he could not remember her hair. He listened with a quiet and a patience he did not know he had, and he thought of his grandfather, of their long nights together fishing not far from there. He remembered how difficult it had been for him to sit so long, and how the stillness of his grandfather had amazed him. Now he understood. It was that his grandfather was old. Listening to the draggers and the drone of the boats, he understood. But he could not remember her hair.

* * * * * * *

His mother knew, in the way that mothers knew such things. Trouble rode the air like one of the pagan goddesses he'd heard of in grade school, not one of the light, bright ones with golden hair and a swept silver gown, but one of the dark beings, misshapen and dwarfed, that the nuns skipped over in the thick green book with the winged horse on its first page.

How did she know? He imagined some disturbance of the air two days before, some shadow that slipped through the light, quick as a cry, that spun through every neighborhood, then swirled down in every mother's, every sister's, every grandmother's ear.

It was crazy. Things were happening to him. He struggled up, stiff with dampness and his hunkering in the shadow of the barge. The fog suddenly lifted, clearing within a minute, and straight ahead of him, no more than fifty feet ashore, two men with their backs to him were drifting downstream in a weathered john boat, smoking. Something under a tarp bulged between them. They turned as one, saw him, started.

"Look," one of them said. The other waved wildly. "Git!" he barked. "Git!"

* * * * * * *

"What do you want to do" he said to Healey, "is to think high. At the end of the board, forget the water. Get all you can from your spring, look up at the height of it, just before you tuck. It's two things, a good dive, and the first is thinking high off the board. The rest is easier then."

"Right," Healey said. "Easier."

He watched Healey wipe out three times. He'd step out to the end of the board, turn, work his heels off at the end. Then, feet together, arms out at his sides, he'd take his spring, throw his head back, and tuck. But he'd freeze each time, instinctively fearing the backwards flip, and in an upside-down jackknife or pike, he'd hit the water shoulder first.

"Get your spring, all of it. Then tuck tighter," he told him. "Then give yourself up to it, man. It'll happen if you give up to it, let it fly. The tuck will get you there, and you'll see the water and know when to come out of it. Look for the water, then plant it."

She'd been watching, smiling. Healey had grinned at her and him, and then, on the next try, he made it all the way around, knifing the water cleanly.

"Oh, yes," Healey said, the water streaming off him as he climbed from the pool. "That felt good."

* * * * * * *

A man came toward him, up out of the river. He held a long cable over his shoulder with both hands. "Know what I got here, boy?" the man said. Water dripped from the end of his nose, from his stubbled chin, from the soaked elbows of his shirt.

He did not answer. The man turned his back to him and began to pull the cable in. He grunted and cursed, as if there were a great weight at the end. He stumbled back, kicking up water. Jacob hunched closer against the barge, his back pressing flakes of rust, his knees wet with the man's splashing. The long gray shank of a grappling hook appeared in the shallows, and in its eye, the knot of the cable gnarled and thick. The man stopped suddenly, turned.

"You know what I got here?" he said.

Jacob nodded.

"Damn right," the man said. He turned back around and jerked the cable one more time. A wavering appeared, just beyond the gray shank of the hook, a floating pool of dull brass, filaments, knots, tangles.

Jacob crouched, tightened, ready to leap.

* * * * * * *

A hand pressed, then softened, on his shoulder. He lifted his head and for a moment the fog was before him again, white, dazzling to his eyes.

"What's the matter?"

"Nothing," he said. His mother looked at him, began to say something, but all that came from her was, "Sleep."

When she was gone, he pushed his chair back from the desk, switched off the light, and felt his way to his bed. He pulled the covers down. He did not undress. He climbed in, pulling the blankets up over his face. It was warm and dark inside, a cave. He did not move. Sometime later he heard his father cough and grumble meanly in his sleep. A mill siren shrilled. When it died, he could hear the trucks across the hollow moaning up Coal Hill, downshifting, then downshifting again, climbing slower and slower, like great beasts burdened with their loads. He lay all night like that, sweating, listening.

Inventing Ironhead

I've been thinking lately about my sons, now that they are both first cousins to language, hugging it awkwardly to themselves and playing with it, prodding it to see what it will do, about how Patrick and Brendan are going to get to know their great-grandfather. Their Pap-Pap's daddy is dead, has been for two decades now, and there is precious little to go on. I think they have only recently come to understand that their grandfather is my dad; how can they comprehend the further increment of relation, the now mute and bodiless notion that "great-grandfather" stands for? They might pause, as I often do, at the top of the back stairs and look at his photograph on the wall. Or they can listen to my stories about him when, in some sidelong and unexpected way, a thought of him arises and I speak it. But none of this will bring him to them truly, not yet, at least. So I write this, in part, to discover how to bring him back, to find the language that will resurrect him, the words that might become him.

"The dead," Norbert Warner writes, "lay claim upon the living and the living honor or dishonor themselves, in part at least, by whether and how they discharge their responsibility to the dead." And Russell Baker says, "We all come from the past, and children ought to know what it was that went into their making, to know that life is a braided cord of humanity stretching up from a long time gone, and that it cannot be defined by the span of a single journey from diaper to shroud."

It is not enough, then, that I have the responsibility of guiding my sons through life, protecting them in their present childhood while preparing them for their futures, but I see now that I am also bound not merely to guide them through but actually to create for them a past.

So with no more plan than this, I begin.

* * * * * *

When I was a boy, my own great-grandmother Maria Madigan (Mu-ry-ah, my father always said, savoring the Gaelic pronunciation: Mu-ry-ah) was still alive. Her house stood on the mill side of South Fourth Street in Steubenville; from the edge of her maple-

shaded backyard, I could look down over the Steubenville Plant of
Wheeling Steel, making smoke in the river bottoms. Its drones and
explosions filled the evenings with the raw material of fire-dreams
and fears. But great-grandma's presence in the parlor, in the huge
stuffed chair by the mantel, was calming, almost hypnotic. Her voice,
her white hair, her great full body that had not wasted with age but
had grown comfortably robust filled the room with a presence and
power. I remember her children, too, though I secretly knew that
the word could never have applied to them, my great-aunts and
great-uncles. They were nine in number, Irish-Catholic in spirit
(which is to say, they prayed the rosary with all the trance-like intensity of Druids, were avidly religious but frequently intolerant,
and trusted the Pope but almost no other authority), and ranging in
temperament from calm to belligerent. I knew and enjoyed them
all. One of those children was Helen, my grandmother—Ironhead's
wife.

I especially remember her and her sisters: Miriam, Dorothy,
Leona (called Nonie) and Mary Kathryn, who I knew for years, before I learned she had any other name, as Aunt Lamb. Only she and
Helen ever married; the others lived together for three-quarters of a
century, tough-minded working women full of prayer and religion
and endless recitations of the histories—public and private—of dozens of Steubenville families. They knew railroaders and mafiosi,
priests and numbers kings, humbugs and politicians. At the slightest mention of some deceased person, they intoned "God rest her
soul" and looked heavenward, just as the nuns had taught them.
They called my father "Jimmy" as if he were still a boy, or they
called him "Firp," a name he was burdened with as a young man
because of his resemblance to the Argentinean boxer Benny Firpo.
At Christmas, they sent crisp five-dollar bills in red, cellophane-
windowed envelopes to my brother and sister and me, and on Sun-
days, after Mass, they sat in the front room and slipped me buffalo
nickels and thin Mercury dimes to spend at Mosblack's Hobby Shop
or at the store a man named Gabriel, who had hair in his ears, kept
next to St. Peter's School.

These women's mother, Maria the calm, Maria the elegant, notable as a member of one of the "pioneer Catholic families" in
Steubenville, as her obituary put it, was born in 1868, just a few
months after Ralph Waldo Emerson delivered a lecture entitled "Social Life in America" in Steubenville. (It was panned, by the way,

in the June 3, 1868 edition of the Steubenville *Herald*.) It is startling to me, but as I write this, I see it must be true: not only was she alive when Emerson was, and Whitman, and Melville, and Twain, but she was born just 71 years after the establishment of Fort Steuben, only 80 years after the opening of the Northwest Territory. The original Land Office for the Northwest Territory is still preserved in Steubenville; George Washington signed some of the earliest deeds. It is not at all impossible that my great-grandmother, that woman who held me in her arms when I was an infant, had been herself as an infant held in the arms of a man who had been present at the establishment of the Fort, or who had been among the earliest settlers, an acquaintance of Washington himself.

A few years ago I spent six weeks in England, studying at Oxford. (What Ironhead would have thought about that one is a mystery to me; what I myself think about it, and about how I, the grandson of this man, wound up there, is equally a mystery). At any rate, I remember my first impressions of the town, and how my nerve was almost broken by the grandness and antiquity of this, the oldest university in England, one of the oldest in the Western world, and in whose Bodleian Library (in existence before Columbus sailed to America) I, the grandson of a fellow whose friends included Hambone McCarthy and Money O'Brien, would sit studying T. S. Eliot and the novels of Thomas Hardy.

And I remember the section of town wall, a thousand years old, at the back of the courtyard of the Turf Pub, in Holywell Street, just a two-minute walk from my college. In America, something manmade and a thousand years old would be in the Smithsonian; in England, it's a backdrop for lunch.

The past in America, at least my personal past, is so much closer, though, so much more tinged with personal significance than the past that almost swallowed me in England. The proximity of my own great-grandmother to the beginnings of my town literally gives me pause. I do not exactly know how to think about it, or how to feel about it, except to be overwhelmed again by what I have felt all my conscious life, and unaccountably so: a chronic, somewhat melancholy nostalgia, bordering on a sense of having been there, somehow, and now being outcast from the past—banished, or lost.

"In Ireland, we've always looked backwards," says Mick Maloney, an Irish immigrant quoted in "Out Of Ireland," an article appearing in *Humanities* magazine recently. He goes on to explain,

"We have a saying that nostalgia...is a thing of the future." Janis Johnson, the interviewer, observes that among many Irish immigrants, "the sense of loss of the idealized vision of the Mother Country...remains pervasive." I know for sure that I have no idealized vision of the Mother Country (more on this later), but I certainly seem to have inherited from somewhere that "sense of loss."

It most frequently manifests itself when I step inadvertently into what I call "holes in time." As a boy, for example, I frequently wandered in the woods down the hillside from my neighborhood. At a fair distance to the northeast lay Beatty Park, a landscape of ancient elms and beeches growing for the sun out of a classic steep-sided Appalachian hollow, with a narrow road winding all the way up it along the creek until at last it opened into Union Cemetery, at the beginning of the town's West End. The hollow, the great trees, the quiet, the cemetery destination of the road — all of these affected me as a boy. I was half-frightened, but not enough to run home; half-drawn, but not enough to recklessly pursue.

Now suddenly it is thirty years later, two hundred and fifty miles away from all that. I am sitting at my desk in Cincinnati, reading William Cooper Howells' *Recollections of Life In Ohio: from 1813 to 1840*, and this passage arises before me: "There is a little valley near Steubenville, to the south-west of the town, and in it I found a near cut from one place to another...Whenever I entered this valley, at either end of it, I was invariably affected by a great dejection of spirits, which lasted until I passed out of it, and whether alone or in company this was always the case. The distance through it was a little less than two miles. There was nothing about this valley, of tradition or peculiarity of situation, that could call up associations, to me at least, of an unhappy kind. But to me it was always a place of melancholy shadows, and it was the only locality that ever so affected me."

There it was: Howells saying, over a century and a quarter before, what I had not quite put into words — and about the exact same place.

Again: I am fifteen or sixteen, and my friends and I are climbing the cliffs across the river from Steubenville. Years before, at the top of this cliff, there had been a dance pavilion and park; the high point was known as Town Rock. We approach the top, looking down on the cars speeding along West Virginia's Route 2, when a small cave opens before us. I crouch and enter, and there, carved into the sandstone, are my own initials, JRH, arranged in the distinctive monogram I've seen my father make a hundred times. When I ask him, later that day, if he'd even been in a cave just below Town Rock when he was a boy, he shrugs. "I don't remember."

Once more: ten or twelve years ago, I wake from a vivid dream, a dream in which I behold Steubenville in its youth, before the coming of the mills. It might be 1820 or 1830. The sun is shining brightly, the air absolutely clear, the river gleaming in its wooded banks, the town clean and orderly with its dwellings and a freshness and simplicity that moves me. I wake with tears on my cheeks. What is it all about?

I told myself that I had dreamed my way back to the town in its childhood, and that what I mourned was not Steubenville's fall from its original Arcadian beauty into its post-Industrial decline, but my own lost youth, my own sooty and ill-smelling and nasty plunge from innocence.

That explanation held up for a long time, until, not long ago, I was wandering around in Howells again, and this suddenly appeared: "When just above Mingo Bottom...I came in sight of [Steubenville] which was prettily built and showed well from that point. It is quite fresh in my memory that it was really beautiful, and as I thought, the most splendid view of my existence." I had again fallen through to the Old Time. I had seen Steubenville as the youthful Howells had, he and his family coming to it for the first time in 1813 from the river.

I am not a mystical person, nor a believer in reincarnation (though a couple of long Oxford lunches with a retired teacher from India named Basil Demel got the hair up on the back of my neck.) But this pattern of "holes in time" means something, and it is connected to the sense of exile and sadness that separates me from my past. And for whatever reason, on my way to Ironhead, I have to pass close to great-grandmother Madigan, and to these stories.

Her uncle — or possibly her brother — these things are not clear to me as yet — fought in the Union Navy during the Civil War. Her maiden name was Scanlon. I have sketchy information suggesting that the Scanlons were born in Ireland, but raised in England. I do not know if it is true. At any rate, Maria Scanlon married John Madigan, whose mother was a Cain, a family either from Rosscommon or County Clare. They held the grocery contract for riverboats in Steubenville; when packets up from Cincinnati and Louisville and Marietta and Wheeling came by, they would row out in john boats laden with vegetables, dry goods, meat and sundries, and do business there, rocking balanced in the middle of the Ohio.

I never knew my great-grandfather Madigan. I do not even know what he did for a living, though my guess is that he was a railroader, since all my other ancestors were—even my maternal grandfather Henry Heights, whose real name, we just recently learned, was Hajec. He came from Poland in the 1930s to work on the Pennsylvania line. But that's another story.

Ken Kesey writes, "It takes the past a long time to happen." This past I am trying to unfold now is only beginning to happen for me, because only now am I beginning to pay more than a passing interest in it. I am trying to set it down in language. Without language of some kind there is, in strictly practical terms, no past. With no words from the past, no names, no journals, no family papers, nothing that reaches into the present, there is no history. The naming of things helps keep them alive.

That's why my older son, Patrick, carries his great-grandfather's middle name: Cavanaugh. As often was the case among the Irish, the middle name of the son was the mother's or grandmother's maiden name. So we gave it to Patrick deliberately, to preserve that thread over the centuries, and to memorialize Ironhead.

Of those Cavanaughs, we have only one brief but poignant story. Margaret Cavanaugh, Ironhead's grandmother, came over from Ireland on a sailing ship in 1837 at the age of four. There was a goat aboard, and its milk sustained her during the voyage. Beyond that, we know next to nothing: a few scattered addresses, a marriage, a death, the story of an heirloom ladle, brought by Margaret's family to America and which my great-grandmother Hague described in a hand-written note to my Uncle Jack when he was boy in the 1930s. So in part, Patrick carries the Cavanaugh name as a burden and responsibility—if we are not able to discover and tell the story, it will be up to him to live into his name and to discover its history and meaning for himself.

So who was this James Cavanaugh Hague, this Ironhead, and what am I to make of his life? He was born on November 14, 1891, just a year before his future wife Helen. He went to St. Peter's School, as his father did, and as great grandmother Madigan did, and I assume he went to high school. (Wrongly so, I learn later: no high school for this working man who sent one son to World War II and then later to an engineer's position in the Bell Telephone Company with no college training but great hard work and tenacity, and two other sons to college — the first American Hagues in our branch of the family to go. And who knows — maybe Uncle Jack and Uncle Paul were the first Hagues ever — either here or in Ireland — to go to university. There should have been a great celebration when Jack matriculated at Ohio State and Paul at Xavier during the war and then later at The College of Steubenville.)

My earliest memories of Ironhead are linked to the river and to the railroad. My grandparents lived at 118 Logan Street when I was a boy, the unmistakable stink of the paper mill less than a couple of hundred yards upriver, fouling the air with roils of rotting cardboard-smelling smoke pouring from its tall silver stack. There was a stone wall in the side yard of their house, topped off with river biscuits — water-rounded loaves of sandstone that turned black as cannonballs in the sulphuric air within a few weeks of being pulled from the water. Behind the house, obscured by the back lawn and a couple of brick-circled flowerbeds, lay the remains of the original homestead which had been torn down before I was born.

I seem to recall a story (or am I inventing?) that from the second floor of the original house my great-grandmother Hague threw all her old furniture, which was promptly burned there in the yard for no other reason than that it "was old." Do I detect a hint of my ancestors' desire to rise from shantyboat to lace curtain Irish in this immolation of a link to an unfashionable — and probably poorer — past?

My grandfather did not seem to be much concerned with class. There was, after all, something leveling about the good salaries paid by unionized industry. As a fireman on the Penn Central Railroad in the summer of my junior year in college, I was asked by more than one old-timer why I wanted to teach school. "You could make more sitting there on that firebox than you could with a college degree. There's two or three brakemen working out there was teachers before, but quit, because the money was better on the railroad."

A story from Ironhead's railroad days. He had the bad luck to be called off the extra board at Mingo Junction on Christmas Eve for a run to Pittsburgh. In our family, Christmas was the highest of high holydays. Not only did we all attend Midnight Mass, but we went again on Christmas Day. So my grandfather, never one too patient with things he hadn't planned himself, set his jaw and went off. The way it was told to me, he took that train to Pittsburgh in record time, dead-headed back to Steubenville, and was at Midnight Mass, bathed, shaven, and decked out in his best suit, with minutes to spare.

But Ironhead never got rich on the railroad, not even close. Long after his death, the subject of his finances came up, and my father allowed as how there had been almost nothing left to grandma. When working with some of his cronies like Hambone McCarthy on the occasional fireman's job I'd get out of Mingo or Weirton Junction, West Virginia, I'd learned that at one time, my grandfather had liked to play the horses. An Irish enough indulgence, this alone would not account for there being little money at his death. Nor did he live extravagantly in any way. He never owned a car. He never went on vacations except to visit his sons and their families, and he had a railroader's pass to pay for that. The living room at 118 Logan Street was furnished with a formidably uncomfortable sofa and two inviting though worn and pipe-scorched leather chairs and a floor lamp. That was about it, save for the Rookwood vase on the mantel, known by all the children in the family as "the penny jar" and whose contents we would pour out onto the floor and count, to pass the time. In the dining room stood a huge console radio that my grandfather listened to the Pirates on, Bob Prince's voice rough as Monongahela rye whiskey on the air, and across from it a glass-doored china cabinet filled with my grandmother's crystal and china. When a train went by, the whole thing rattled and tinkled like a huge wind chime. Where did his money go? Who knows? Maybe it took even more than two generations to recover from the original Irish poverty.

But whatever the financial status of the family, Ironhead, when he "went downtown" (or, of course, to Mass), was always a natty dresser. A dandy of the old school, he wore pin-stripes, suspenders, white shirt, and, over his spade-broad wingtips, spats. It occurs to me that not many would know what spats are. According to my *Funk & Wagnall's*, a spat is "a short gaiter worn over a shoe and fastened underneath with a strap." The word is usually used in the plural: "spats," and is short for "spatterdash." The original use for spats long gone (all the streets my grandfather commonly traveled in Steubenville were paved) he ran no risk, outside of flood season, of ruining his shoes in the water and mud. But he wore them nevertheless, even into the Sixties, and so did his cronies, especially at Mass. They brought an odd, antique touch to dress-up occasions, and gave us something interesting to consider when our minds wandered from Monsignor Grigsby's sermons.

The conservatism implicit in the wearing of those spats, however, reveals another side of Ironhead, a stubborn hard-headedness, an unwillingness to change, a tenacious hanging on to what he had fought for and earned.

One of the most vividly memorable days in my boyhood illustrates something of this tenaciousness, this energy, however sometimes misplaced and unfortunate its manifestations might have been in relations with other social and ethnic groups. I must have been little older than ten, which places this summer day's long journey in 1957 or so. Could he have been 66 years old when we did this? It seems incredible that he would have been so robust even then, but it must have been so.

We started out on a hot summer morning, misty, the West Virginia hills across the river barely visible through the haze and glare. There would have been the smell of the paper mill heavy that morning, and most certainly the background stink of sulphur that pervaded the town during damp summer or winter days. At first, we turned our backs to the river and walked up Logan Street, but quickly went left, to head south on Third Street, parallel to the river. We must have walked right past the spot where the house Ironhead had been born in stood, almost on the bank, a little brick dwelling the likes of which you see all up and down the Ohio Valley in the older sections of towns, and which in my family we call, not very excitingly, "river houses." Soon we came to the Market Street Bridge, and he turned to me and said, "We're going to walk across, Nudnick." (That was Ironhead's endearment for little ones; Yiddish in origin, I think, although it could also be a mis-take on the Latin "quid nunc" — meaning "know-it-all." Whatever, who knows the story of its entry into the intimate vocabulary of a clan of stern Irish Catholics?) But I remember still the excited clenching in my bowels when he announced our project: walking across the river! Now there was an adventure.

The Market Street Bridge was an example of what I have since heard called a "singing bridge." Its deck was of the same steel grid that temporary landing strips were made of in the Second World War: incredibly strong, relatively light, and mostly air — a screen of rubber-polished metal through which you could look down, giddy and unsteady, to the river a hundred feet below. The tires of the cars and trucks crossing it set up a high whine, and the acceleration and slowing of the traffic across it, punctuated by the metallic clash of its joints, audible all through downtown, was another part of the complex music compounded of mill sirens, furnace tappings, the heavy couplings and uncouplings of trains and the hiss and grind of auto traffic that filled the consciousness so completely that once you got out in the country, in some mossy, leaf-muffled hollow, you were uneasy, wary: too quiet. It took us probably little more than five or ten minutes to walk across, me pausing to lean through the iron to spit, watching the tiny white dot weave and veer in the breeze and finally evaporate and disappear long before it hit the water. There was a traffic light on the West Virginia end of the bridge; we waited until it gave us the right of way then jogged across the muddy West Virginia Route 2, still in those days heavily traveled by coal trucks. It was not the usual slag or gravel there along its berm at the foot of the roadcut; it was coal, battered by traffic into a dust that swirled and glinted when a car blew by. It was as deep and as soft underfoot as the sand on the banks of the river, and we made heavy-footed haste to get off the dangerous side of the road. Soon my grandfather turned abruptly left, I followed, and within a steep twenty steps, we paused to look down now on the traffic, the coal trucks and cars and pickup trucks with tools and odd scraps of lumber and hounds sprawled in their beds roaring by toward Weirton, upriver, or Follansbee, downriver. Then we made our slow way up the muddy haul-road that had been blasted into the rock, headed into a place of greenery, mist, and water that Ironhead called Fairy Glen.

In the first grade at St. Peter's the nuns took us, single file and silently, down several flights of narrow stairs into a big room in the basement of the school. There, next to the huge furnace and boiler, music classes gathered. Sister Malachy, her thin face so ruddy she must have rubbed it with sand every morning, stood before us, arms aloft, black rosary looped and clicking at her side. And in between stern rehearsals of the Kyrie and the Agnus Dei, she taught us "The Wearing Of The Green."

> O Paddy dear and did you hear
> The news that's going around:
> The shamrock is forbid by law
> To grow in Irish ground.

That song, banned by British authorities in Ireland because of its connection to the IRA, must have been sung by Ironhead, too, taught to him by his generation's avatar of Sr. Malachy. I try to imagine him sitting there with the squirming Gaughans and Corrigans and Doyles and Joyces and Madigans and McDonoughs of his time, but it is difficult. I know only one story of his boyhood, of witnessing a woman burned to death on the river bank across from Logan Street as the result of an accident with a navigation light; beyond that, no gossip or legend has trickled down. It's not surprising, though, now that I think about it: I didn't even know he bore the name Ironhead until I was in college. To call him that to his face, it was said, simply would not do. In all the meals I ate in their dining room, the china cabinet shivering and glinting at one end, the rich ham loaf my grandmother had cooked now steaming on the buffet, Ironhead's rare, sharp laugh—in all of this, there was never any guest outside of family in attendance. Life was very private there, and to my knowledge not even Ironhead's railroad cronies set foot in his living room. I've always wondered about that, speculating that there must have been some customary or cultural taboo at work, rather than just a kind of peculiar insulation. Or maybe Grandma Hague wouldn't allow it—I just don't know. But what I do know is that along with the religious fervor, Irishness manifested itself the most in a ready anger among many— but by no means all of—the men, in a narrow but intransigent intolerance, and in an attitude that demanded conformity—to the union, the church, the school, the family, the ethnic identity. Among the women, it was manifested in service—to family and church first of all, and then to the country. Helen's sister Miriam worked for the government, and Dorothy was a nurse. Nonie— Aunt Leona—in the words of my father, "kept house." So only in brilliant and unpredictable flashes did the verbal and intellectual side of their Irishness show forth in curt, understated but colorfully fatal dismissals and insults, in the wild bantering of brothers and cousins, in certain afternoons or evenings of reminiscence shading over into story-telling. But the subject matter was never Ireland, never the Old Ways. Some profound amnesia had struck my entire family on the matter of its ancestors, and I had only the sketchiest notions of the European past. The Hague version of Back Then was almost totally set in America, and cast in the American tongue.

So no matter how much I would like to say that as Ironhead and I, that long walking afternoon, lingered in an Appalachian hollow which in name and in atmosphere might well have been some Irish fairy-ground, and no matter how much I can wish now that he had told me stories of Ireland, of Finn MacCool and Fergus, and Cuchulian, and of my own ancestors, survivors all of them, the fact is, he didn't. He was not a man easy with small talk, not among us children, at least, and his Irishness was of a workaday, literal kind, not so much an ethnic as a kind of practical social identity. This was long before the time of Identity Politics; the only politics that mattered then were pro-union and Democratic. I don't know—perhaps he was even a bit defensive of his Irishness, and his occasional ugly dismissals of other groups was one of its symptoms. That day in Fairy Glen, surrounded by a green filtered light and the sound of the creek running down the mountain toward the river, he might have asked me if I knew what kind of fern that was over there, or what kind of beetle it was that glinted and flashed on a rock beyond his foot. But mostly, he would have left me to my own sensations, my own thoughts, and after a time, he would have stood up and said, "Let's move on, Nudnick," and we would have.

But there was certainly a spirit common to Irish culture evident in Ironhead's unsophisticated delight in birds and animals. And there was a proprietary quality to his delight as well; both he and my father were inveterate builders of bird-houses, and from the very beginning of my experience, fishing was an act of conservation and use, not an idle amusement: you ate what you caught or your threw it back, or you took it home and fertilized the garden with it—no wasting allowed. This appreciation of things just for their beauty and grace and rareness seems to me, looking back, one of the sources of the sense of wonder I had as a child about the world of creation, its knowns and its unknowns. Though it must have been obscured by his industrial environment and his life of work among machines, I think Ironhead still retained a Celtic sense of the mystery and intricacy of life, a sense reflected in the elaborate serpentines of Celtic art, and perhaps for him and his cronies, in the pre-Vatican II ornateness of Roman Catholic ritual.

Cronan T. Molloy, pastor of St. Peter's when Ironhead died, delivered an intense eulogy that I thought at the time must have torn the heart out of my grandmother. I know it hauled and rooted at mine, though my own marriage had ended almost exactly at that time, coming down upon me like a collapsing shanty. So who knows what the sources and amplifications of my grief? But Monsignor Molloy's exclamations that "Here was a man!" did inspire in me a simple proud sorrow that I could wear in public later at the graveyard, and that enabled my grandmother at last to recover and to mourn with a heads-up stoicism. But really his death shook me in its sickening commonness: I visited him in the last days only once, sitting by the oxygen tent he lay under, his hand in my father's, his skin pallid and flecked. This was not the god of my boyhood; this was a sick old man whose eyes were closed, and who, instead of the humid moist green of Fairy Glen or the spangled night sky over our fishing spot along the river, was surrounded by a mechanical air fluttering the plastic around him. He could not escape the machines. He could not get back to the hills and dairies and stone fences and trout of Rosscommon, or Clare, or Dingle, or wherever it was we're from. He couldn't even get back to the river bank at the foot of Logan Street. Not to his coal cellar nor the basement to feed the furnace. Not to St. Peter's to stand on the front steps with his spats and pinstripes on. Not to sit on the porch swing at night hearing the nighthawks beep over the papermill. Such a situation was simply unsatisfactory: it wouldn't do. I walked out of the hospital into the night air that reeked of sulphur and wood pulp. After a while, I decided not to cry.

Bike

In the summer of 1961, my neighborhood awoke from its calm and pedestrian childhood into the Age of the Motorbike. Three of my friends almost simultaneously acquired Mopeds, small motorized sleeknesses with voices like cicadas which they buzzed incessantly up and down the street until my heart constricted with envy.

Buying one myself was out of the question. I was fourteen, only just beginning to work occasional Saturday morning jobs for sixty-five cents an hour. The several hundred dollars that a Moped would cost were light-years away. But when I watched Petey Visnic and Aldo Isidore and Chuck Humes speed by, festooned like knights in the blue streamers of their exhaust, a wanderlust struck me. I too wanted to go like that. On such a machine, I could climb the steep hills of Steubenville, raise dust across the abandoned strip mine, hum out the cemetery gates beyond it. I could fly by the high school I was about to enroll in, on out past it all into adventure, powerful and free.

And so with Joey Pierro, another neighborhood boy who lacked capital, I decided to build my own motorbike. Some time before, in an illegal hillside dump near the strip mine, I'd found the wreckage of an old motorcycle. It was a pre-World War II model known as a "Whizzer." Rather than a chain or driveshaft, the Whizzer ran by means of a long belt attached to a pulley on the engine crankshaft at one end, and seated in a flange welded to the rim of the twenty-inch rear wheel at the other. A clutch engaged the belt by friction; when the rider let it out, the belt tightened on the rim-flange, and off he went.

But I had no motor. And even then, as illiterate a mechanic as I was, I knew that I needed not just any motor, but one with a horizontal shaft. It had struck me that a lawn mower engine, of one-and-a-half or two horsepower, might do the trick. But most lawn mowers had vertical-shaft engines, and if turned on their sides would flood or stall or even catch fire. My father, however, had an old one with a Briggs & Stratton horizontal-shaft engine on it, and after several weeks' dickering, he gave in and let me have it.

Joey and I shagged a wheel-less 20-inch bike from his basement and went to work. We needed to build a frame to mount the engine on, right behind the seat, and we needed to make it sturdy enough to handle the torque and vibration the engine would produce. For three days we noodled the problem, sitting on the rock wall lining Joey's driveway, the Whizzer wheel, the Briggs & Stratton, and the old bike arranged opposite us like the equipment for some physics experiment. After scratching several plans, we finally went to a junkyard and bought five feet of two-inch angle iron to build the motor frame with. We spent several days cutting the pieces by hand with an old hacksaw. We raised blisters on our fingers and palms, bitter sweat stung our eyes, and iron filings got inside our shirts and itched us all day. We felt powerful, magnificent.

Our mothers worried when they learned of our project, and lobbied our fathers to forbid us to ride such a dangerous thing. Our fathers, I suspect, did not think we'd get it built. They counted on our enthusiasm waning as the work got more difficult; as we encountered problems or lacked tools, they thought, we'd be stumped and then we'd quit.

But they had forgotten what it is to be a boy, to have a long summer of twelve-hour, uncommitted days, and most of all, they had forgotten how powerful the need for breaking away could be. Joey and I kept ourselves going through a month's work by imagining the speed and power the bike would bring to us. We imagined our changed lives, no longer confined to the ridgetop our neighborhood occupied; we imagined the wind cool on our faces on hot August afternoons as we glided down Market Street Hill, a part of the traffic, a part of the flow of real life that up until then we'd only stood by and cautiously watched from the curb. We would be able to go, at will, anywhere we wanted, and the thrilling promise of that fed our work. We slaved willingly at building that bike. The more we worked at it, the more we wanted it. It was a self-sustaining reaction.

Not that everything was easy. For example, after cutting the frame for the engine mount, we had to drill fourteen holes through that quarter-inch thick iron in order to bolt it all together and to attach it to the bike. We burned out two electric drills in the process, and several thousand nerves cells each as well. I still remember the shrill grinding of the bits into the iron, still feel the handle of the drill pressing into my chest as I leaned against it, afraid that the bit would snap again, as it did twice, under the heat and pressure, gashing my hand.

Tools, we learned, could be dangerous if misused, if pressed beyond their right use or capacity. And inanimate matter—iron and drill bits, for example—was obstinate, frustrating. Things simply would not become what you wanted them to become. Their shaping took time and work, even drudgery and pain. There were, we came to realize, no short cuts. There was no magic. Sweat and skill, however hard-earned, through whatever hard knocks, through trial and error after error—persistence and keeping the end always in mind—these were the real requirements, the hard, good lessons.

During the last week of June we finished the motor mount. The two of us lifted the engine into place, feeling a grand satisfaction that the holes we'd drilled lined up with the holes of the bottom of the engine. Proudly, we bolted it fast. Then we leaned the bike against the driveway wall, the motor jutting a foot and a half above and slightly to the right of the seat, and we admired. We did not see how ungainly and ugly the bike was, nor did we give a moment's thought to how dangerous it might be to ride something so top-heavy and so frail. The Briggs & Stratton far outweighed the light bike frame; we hadn't even considered that its weight, suspended so far back over the rear axle, might pull the front tire up off the ground and so make steering impossible. We were blind to all that—the thing was a triumph: a masterpiece.

Nor, in that marvelous instant in which the near-finished bike first stood before us, did we much worry that it lacked both a clutch and brakes. We'd removed the original coaster brakes from the rear wheel in order to make room for the uprights of the motor mount, which were bolted to the ends of the axle. We'd been anxious about this shortcoming for a time, but gradually, as our excitement to finish the bike overcame us, we rationalized it away by agreeing that we were, in this little enterprise, engaged in the business of going, not stopping. We had also, in a little thought-experiment before we'd ever mounted the engine, concluded that the compression of the engine itself, if the choke were all the way out, might help to slow the bike to a relatively safe, foot-assisted halt.

The clutch, too, had been a problem. Given the way the engine was mounted, it would be impossible to raise or lower it to loosen or engage the belt. Nor was there room on the small bike frame itself to rig a workable clutch. It was an all-power or no-power situation; we decided, of course, on all. There would be no clutch. Rather, the rider would pull the choke all the way out and run alongside as the engine turned over. Then he would jump into the seat, at the same time reaching back to jam the choke in, and hang on as the bike lurched ahead. It would be awkward, dangerous, crazy. And as seasoned tough guys by now, used to the fumes of gasoline and hot iron, our hands scarred with gouges and cuts, we took pride in it: another difficulty to master.

On the other hand, we had figured out a workable throttle over the last two days. Scavenging some brake and gear cables from an old English racing bike, we'd rigged a method of accelerating by twisting a plastic grip on the right side of the handlebars: the cable attached to the engine throttle simply wound around it. To slow down, the rider reversed the twist; a small spring on the Briggs & Stratton pulled the cable back.

We flipped for the inaugural ride: Joey won. His first trip was a nervous single orbit around the block, but the grin he wore when he jerked the bike to a rough stall in the driveway matched any stunt-driver's after a show. "Damn, damn, damn," he said, pale with fear and excitement. "It works."

And then, something strange and unforeseen developed. Joey and I rode the bike for the next full week, rode it for hundreds of miles, cruising along with our friends on their Mopeds, basking in their half-wry, half-admiring gazes. But we never once left the neighborhood. Never once did we descend the long, winding hill leading down from our ridge into town, into the "real" world, the far away. For all our dreams of freedom, when the opportunity was at hand, when we could have taken off and driven away, we hung back, close to home. Some vague unease broke our nerve.

Looking back from more than thirty years' distance now, I am beginning to understand that unexpected hesitation. For the first time in our young lives, we had consciously made a choice to break away — from our neighborhood, ringed by hollows which at once isolated and protected us, from our parents, from the familiar site of our own swiftly ending childhoods. More profoundly, we had accomplished this possibility on our own, through our own design and hard work, through the power of our own minds. We had shaped a new world deliberately, opened it up in what for two boys was a quantum leap, and as the realization of that tremendous fact sank in, we instinctively stepped back from it. We were wary of what our own cleverness had wrought.

It has become for me a private parable. Joey and I had produced a machine whose power we had not imagined clearly through to the end, for all our careful planning. Though muddled together by two boys not yet old enough to shave, that motorbike was bigger than we were. And though we eventually overcame our fears—*o felix culpa*—and though we did, indeed, ride that bike out into the world, down Market Street Hill in the noon-hour rush, to the cursing and amazed shouts of drivers all around us, and to great peril to our own safety, I have not forgotten that week of circling home and childhood and innocence, nor the anxieties and uncertainties it produced.

The life of every child has its turning points, its sudden spurts of growth to new levels of knowledge, achievement, experience, even sad wisdom. So too, I think, do the lives of towns and nations. Unwittingly, Joey and I had re-enacted, in our small, tinkering way, the history of Steubenville itself as it had changed, a little more than a century before, from a pastoral community of sheepfolds and agrarian simplicity into an industrialized company town, dark with soot and new wealth, powerful and nearly self-destructive with the technologies of steel.

And I do not think that it would be going too far to say that we had foreshadowed another critical point, of national and potentially planetary impact as well. For it was to be only a bit more than a year from that summer, as a student in the high school I'd dreamed of riding the bike by, that I sat numb in Sister Eunice's English class while the principal, over the loud-speaker, reported in a shaky voice the unfolding nuclear confrontation between Soviet-backed Cuba and the United States. In faraway places like Omaha, Nebraska and Langley, Virginia and Washington, D.C; in Havana, and Moscow, and Vladivostok, some boys had been playing with their clever machines, and they had suddenly found them bigger, more powerful than they liked. And they were afraid.

Death In the Afternoon

To the neighborhood boys, it was known as Walker's Pond. Like Indian Rock and Fox's Den, it had become one of those sacred sites to which all of us, in our random, self-induced initiations, had made pilgrimage. To get there, we trudged uphill and uphill to the top of the ridge our neighborhood clung to, then up again, out across the abandoned strip mine with its bulldozer ruts and the set of wrecked caterpillar tracks that jutted from a spoilbank like iron fossils. Nothing grew on that slaughtered expanse save a few bristly clumps of broom sedge and a stunted locust sapling that had somehow taken root in the acid debris. There was no topsoil.

Along the edge of the surviving woods, swathes of goldenrod blazed in ditches, their temporary bloom fed by the rotting trunks of trees pushed over the hill by the mining machines. But the top was as barren as a desert. To my innocent eyes, that rocky waste was interesting, even beautiful, for all its contrast with the closed-in vistas of the hollows and wooded ridges my end of town wandered through. There was no place else in my world where I could see so much of the sky.

It was more of a thoroughfare than a place we lingered in, though. A dusty haul road wound all the way across it and finally plunged in a series of rugged switchbacks down to the paved surface of Coal Hill. Where this road began its descent, the pond lay at the bottom of a deep depression in a meadow, green with scum, and surrounded by a fringe of cattails. In the spring, we could hear its voice from afar, a high shrill of peepers on the damp wind.

The pond had escaped pollution from the mine by some miracle. Its water bred newts, leopard and bull frogs, toads, and provided habitat for queen snakes, redwing blackbirds, and a multitude of aquatic insects. Still, the mud of its bottom was a suspicious black under a few inches of brown sediment, and smelled faintly of oil.

In a region of swift-running waters—the Ohio River and all the upland runs and creeks and seeps that coursed down to it through the hills and hollows—the pond was a rare stillness. But it gathered in its green patience a furor of vitality, as if all the life displaced by the mine had concentrated itself there for one last stand.

One May, descending the steep pasture slope, the collapsing Walker farmhouse just visible for a moment over a distant rise, we found ourselves in the midst of a strange migration. With each step we took, gaggles of toads leaped aside, burping their garbled croaks as if stuck with shivs. At the pond's edge, a thousand of them gathered in a gross exultation, indiscriminately humping and squirming in mud. When at last we realized what their game was, we lost our senses. Horror and disgust bred in us a vicious glee. Arming ourselves with sticks, we waded through those breeding clumps, swatting and crunching, until our shoes and jeans glistened with blood and egg-slime, and the air filled with a raw meat smell that finally sickened us. Collapsing on the pond's northern edge, we lay a long hour in a kind of half-repentance. I do not know exactly what we thought, nor how we felt, nor what awful lesson we had taught ourselves. Even in such vivid moments, mystery often spreads its dark cape before and behind us, and we cannot see.

There were two boats at the pond, actually the torched-off hoods of old cars, window pillars left on; to us, they looked enough like the high-prowed ships of Vikings to inspire war at sea. We'd pole our ways out, smashing the cattail clumps where the blackbirds built their nests, and jab our pikes at one another, shouting and thrusting until we all had been unshipped. We raised such commotion for hours, whipping the pond into a froth of brown algae foam and littering its surface with broken leaves. Then we would lie on the grass of the slope and wolf down our waterlogged lunches of pepperoni and cheese while the trash on the pond drifted in the breeze and the blackbirds creaked and worried in the ruins.

One languid afternoon, I left my drowsing friends ashore and poled out into the pond alone. The bottom of the boat was warm to my bare feet. I took off my shirt and sat down. The thin steel of the car hood gave beneath me. As I lay back, my head rested almost at the level of the water.

I saw something drifting toward me. It was pink, an alien color in that place of mud and scum. Turning my head to one side, I watched it pass in slow motion, less than a foot away. Suddenly, the day pressed in upon me, suffocating and bitter, as if I'd been buried under a dozer's load of hot soil. There on the surface, a giant water bug struggled up out of its nymph's skeleton, which lay like a ghost behind it on the water. Its great grasping forelegs, like hinged scythes, waved in the air; it labored to pull itself free of its youth. But its body was broken. Its head and thorax had been ripped almost completely away from its abdomen in our morning's roughhousing. So now the legs pushed against the remains of its demolished end. Pale, infirm, unsettling for all its ruined predatory power, it pulled itself in two before my eyes, a few strands of its intestines stretched and breaking over the air of its parting.

The breeze that had steered this catastrophe toward me died down. The water bug stalled before me. I lay motionless for five, ten minutes there, watching its death. From where my friends loafed in the grass ashore, it must have appeared that I had fallen asleep. I could hear their murmuring and laughing, and the buzz of katydids, and the loose-shutter clatter of grasshoppers flying in the meadow above. Silently, the water bug slowed its struggle; at last it was still. My neck and shoulders cramped with my own stillness.

The rest of that afternoon at the pond is a blank, a forgotten dream. But at its end, as we walked home across the mine, I remember realizing how large the sky was, how oppressive and faceless, and how the clumps of broom sedge, each one of them, seemed now to mark a small grave. It was good to descend into my neighborhood again, to run deliberately into the shadows of the great calm elm in front of my house, among accustomed places and orderly events: the smell of supper on the air, the shouts of children on the corners, the safe, familiar buzz of the lawn mower in the yard next door. It was good to stop there, catching my breath, never looking back.

Needles

His skin wasn't green, exactly. You think of old Christmas trees, out in the snow in the middle of January, waiting for the trash man to take them, maybe, but that wasn't it. Or you think of the pond where you used to shoot frogs as a kid—the water scummy and fuzzed, the B-B gun splatting out its little copper cusses against the frogs' wallet-slick skin. But that wasn't it either. It was a hospital ward green, the basement of your old grade school green. Fluorescent lights on the backs of cheap plastic binders the color of faded Clorets. Poor nutrition. Bad times as a kid. That kind of green.

But it wasn't any illness anybody knew about. That's the main fact. There didn't seem to be any ordinary thing wrong with the man. You'd watch him go three days without sleeping, drinking coffee by the quart, smoking a pack of cigarettes in an hour sometimes, and still going strong, telling jokes, muscling the heaviest coils of tinplate in the mill.

"Needles!" the foreman yelled at him one day last week. "You either take a day off and get some sleep, or I'll write you up on a safety violation."

Needles limped over and looked at him, his face like a spoiled moon over a pit of chlorine, his eyes black as No. 9 coal. "You do that, Ernie, I'll break your back."

We drank beer together that night at the Smokestack. Across Sixth Street the winos loafed in front of Pug's Hotel. The 11:40 highballed through to Pittsburgh, paper and leaves swirling like dust devils aross the station lot. Needles shuddered at that, lost the thread of what he was saying.

A little later he picked it up. "It's because they're all soft inside," he said. "Ernie and Zambini and the rest of them. Management. Them yellow hard hats they wear tell the story: they ain't nothing but mashed bananas in their heads. The whole gang ain't worth dirt."

I drifted off then myself. Sometimes Needles did that to you. Something he'd say would set off a whole string of dreams and angers in your head. You'd stored them up for months, years, and maybe even convinced yourself you'd gotten over them.

But then you'd sit down over a beer with Needles, and he'd start in on it, and they'd all come back.

"Needles," I said a little while later. "When did you eat last?" He thought. "I don't think I've eat for a week," he said finally. "It's a waste of time."

Somebody found him down on Water Street a couple of days later. It was like he'd blown up. Binkiewicz the cop was the man on the case, he lives upstairs of me and tells the whole story. The car nothing but scrap metal. Guts everywhere. A finger on a windowsill half a block away. Three teeth stuck in a perfect straight line in the trunk of a cottonwood down on the river. "Mafia all the way," Binkiewicz says. "Quick and dirty and expensive."

It wasn't the Mafia. It was his mother. In a way, it was Needles's mother made him blow up.

She'd died twenty years earlier, but she still shaped his life, the memory of her like a train wreck in his sleep. I loved the man, but I couldn't cure him; I couldn't love him enough. But she had loved him more than her own heart. And she'd busted her heart for him, and him only twelve, and it was the only love he ever'd ever felt. He stuck there in his notion of love, never got any further.

He was sitting on the tracks outside their shanty, and a train was coming, and Needles had gotten his foot twisted in the space between a loose tie and the rail. Just like in the Saturday matinees, only this wasn't a movie, not a movie at all. His mother heard him screaming over the train, and she ran out, and she pulled and pulled, and at last the little bones in Needles's ankle broke, and he fell over her, over on top of his mother who was dead, finished that moment in her work and fear. Her eyes looked straight up without blinking as the reefers and coalcars stormed by and Needles lay on the cinders with his one foot strange and bent beneath him.

So Needles lived — he lived hard — to pay her back. Worked at the mill through his twelve weeks' vacation, time-and-a-half, doubled up whenever he could, worked sixteen, eighteen hours at a shot, eight off, then back on, filled in for guys on sick leave. He was worth a fortune, and it was all his mama's. He lived like a mouse in a basement room of Pug's, hardly ate, and had ten thousand more hours than anyone with his years of service.

And he just blew up. It wasn't the Mafia. It was Needles and his mama and something dark inside him as a train roaring down and not killing him but taking away his mama. It was too much for him, and he finally got out of it as quickly as he could. He blew up. I know it. People can do these things when they have to.

Three or four bosses came to the funeral. They stood in the back porch of the Funeral Home and smoked. The casket was closed. There was a picture of Needles on the wall behind it, framed by a bunch of angry yellow flowers. There were a couple of women weeping. Nobody knew who they were, maybe aunts from out of town somewhere.

I got the funeral director aside, a man named Diver. "Listen," I said. "I don't know exactly how to ask this, but was he green all over? I mean what was left. Like his face—was he all green?"

There was this disease going around, real hush-hush. Covered up by the mill. Nobody knew the facts.

Diver looked toward the back porch where the bosses stood. Then he stared at me. He was a pale man with skin so thin you could see through it. His teeth were crooked. He had three blond hairs in his nose.

"I knew things were bad in this town." he said. "But I didn't know they were sick. You should see a doctor. And I don't mean a podiatrist." He pointed at his head. "Maybe it was contagious," he said, laughing nervously. "All you guys asking these weird questions about the deceased."

"Look," I said. "I don't give a shit about what you think. I want to know if the man was green."

Diver raised his eyebrows. "Ain't everybody?" he said. "I mean ain't everybody around here a little green? What do you think, you live in East Jesus or something, apple trees on the lawn? This is a mill town. What I've seen would make you throw up."

"Was he green?" I said.

"Yes," he said.

"That's funny," I said.

"What's funny?" he said.

"Look at your hands."

He looked. I left him looking. He turned them over, as I walked out, looking at his own hands out in front of him like they were things he'd never seen before.

Out back I stood with the bosses and had a smoke. A little devil in a big-time hell. When I left they were talking about Needles. They were talking about him and his mother and his bankroll. The edges of their lips were green.

You think of bad wheels turning, slick briefcases opening, judges and hard, hungry juries. Then think of money that's changed hands a thousand times, all the palm grease smearing the printing. That kind of green.

Breaking

"Goddama you breakin em."

Saturday morning, a February mean with ice, and I'm helping unload the truck. The driver's everything I know about Chicago, talks funny, wears cowboy boots and a Stetson. He carries a gun, an old long-barreled revolver, jammed down the back of his pants so it rests in the crease of his butt. Name's Clarence.

"Goddama you breakin em."

That's Primo Guerrero, head cutter. Quick with a knife as he is with a woman. He doesn't help us unload; he comments. We're nothing but a bunch of trouble to him, high school punks.

At first you can feel your hands freezing. There's an ache that runs up your fingers, the bones in them, right up the center of each one. But then that goes away. And that's when you're in trouble. You drop the hindquarter and maybe smash your buddy's hand, but he doesn't know it for an hour, and then he fucks this and fucks that all day, trying to make a fist but he can't. So maybe he punches the wall in the john, right under the picture of the naked woman, and that makes it easier for him somehow.

I used to run track. The mile, 880. I liked to get out in front of everybody, sprinting right out, the sound of the others fading behind me. Getting away, breaking out of the pack. That felt good. But this work has killed my knees. The bottom of the trailer is an inch of cold grease and running the sides and quarters down you slip about half the time and go down on the grooves of the floor. Three or four bad ones like that and your knees are gone.

"Goddama, boys, you breakin em."

What we're breaking is Primo's balls. He stands below the rollers and checks the quarters and sides and the boxes of bacon and the barrels of Calais hams off the invoice. If just two boxes back up he grabs his crotch through his bloody apron and he cries, "Goddama you breakin em!" We don't work fast enough for him. He's the boss's head honcho, always in a hurry.

After we get the truck unloaded Clarence comes back from the Twilight. That's the bar next door. He still doesn't talk to us. He only speaks to the boss out front, and they only talk numbers. I mean the racket. The boss is one of two or three hotshots in the numbers here, and we all give him our nickels and dimes or quarters and our picks, straight or boxed. We write them down on pieces of butcher paper around lunch time, and he takes them down the street and comes back with the winnings, if there are any. Me, I've lost maybe a hundred in the two years I've worked here. But one of the clerks, Tina's her name, a skinny woman with glasses who takes care of the lunchmeat case, she hit for three thousand last year the week before Christmas. Threw a big party for us Christmas Eve. Got every one of us high school kids drunk on rye whiskey and Coke. Dominic Antonucci, he's in school with me, spilled half a fifth down the grinder when he was making hamburger. I'd like to have seen one of them burgers hit the skillet. Probably went up like dynamite.

I suppose it's pretty good to have a job. I get out of school at 1:30. They let anybody with a job out early, and I ride the bus downtown and have twenty minutes before I have to show up at the market. I hang around McCrory's, buy a dime's worth of their roasted Spanish peanuts and stand inside the glass front door and eat them while they're still hot from the roaster. There's a big radiator on the wall and it's always warm. Almost everybody in town walks by that door in a day. There's lots to watch.

Take the Chief, for instance. Story is he was a famous football player for Big Red years ago. Scored a couple hundred touchdowns or something and could have played for the Steelers right out of senior year. But he killed a guy down on Lake Erie Avenue, just beat him to death. He got off, but something had broken inside him after that and so now he just bums around, wearing army surplus coats, cleaning windows and sweeping out bars. He's big, with a broad flat face, thick black hair. Never wears a hat. Lots of days all he does is walk Fourth Street from the North End to the South End, back and forth, panhandling cigarettes and quarters.

So I watch till two and then walk down to work. It's just a hole in the wall place, really, from the outside. But inside, it's deep, the cases running all along one side for fifty feet or so and then sweeping around across the back. Behind them are the saws, two of them, beyond a counter about shoulder high where the boss stands looking out over the floor and smoking his cigars. Then there's the door to the room where the cooler is and the cutting tables, and the big sinks where the beginners do their job, which is to wash the meat trays with the green disinfectant that comes in cardboard tubes that weigh about a thousand pounds. They come on the truck, too.

When you first start working here, you bag, out front. There's a conveyor belt under the tables behind the counter, and on a busy Saturday after payday, three or four hundred big sacks of meat come down that. The customers line up with their half of the green register ticket, and the bagger matches the numbers on their tickets to the other half taped to the bags and hands them over. Genius work. The boss counts any mistakes and if there's too many, or if he gets a few phone calls from some old lady whose head cheese is missing, or who has ten pounds of neck bones instead of ten pounds of kielbasa, he fires you. But if you do a pretty good job out there, you can get an extra dime an hour and break in as a clerk, or sometimes you go back and wash the trays.

"Goddama, Dominic, you breakin em."

Dominic is washing the trays and he's just dropped a whole stack. Sounds like a car wreck. Primo jumps and almost cuts himself. His face gets red, redder than his apron. Cutting yourself is the worst thing that can happen to a butcher. It's bad form. When I first started a guy named Foster worked here, he was a drinker, hands shaking all morning till he hit his vodka at lunch time. One morning he sliced the end of his thumb off, half an inch. It fell in among the hamburger trimmings. Primo cussed and made Foster call a cab, telling him he wasn't going to lose time taking some asshole to the hospital. By the time he got back, the other cutters had found the end of his thumb and they'd put it in a matchbox and wrapped it in butcher paper and written Foster's address on it. One of them mailed it on his lunch break. Foster came to work with a gun the day his thumb came in the mail and the boss fired him even before he'd gotten his coat off.

So Primo's mad at Dominic now and throws his trimming knife across the room and it sticks in the wall about a foot from Dominic's head. Dominic stands up from gathering the spilled trays and tells Primo to fuck himself and his brother and three cousins.

The lading bill's checked off now and we've got to stow the boxes of wieners and six barrels of hams in the cooler. The sides and quarters are hanging on the rails behind the cutting blocks and Primo and Tony Cline, a young cutter from the vocational school who's just starting out, begin breaking them. Primo's expert at it, can break a whole side in three swift cuts without thinking. Tony's slower, more careful. Still he messes up once in a while and ruins a piece and Primo stares at him. "Jesµs Christ, Tony," he says. "You breakin em."

It's about 38 or 40 degrees in the cooler and always damp. You wear gloves and stocking caps but still you're cold all through. Just when you're starting to thaw out from unloading the truck, and your hands and feet are coming back to life and aching, you've got to spend an hour in the cooler stacking and pulling.

I knew this girl once, Carmen DeLucca. She was tall and skinny but beautiful, hair the color of olive oil. She had hard little breasts and said the Hail Mary to herself whenever I touched them. We went out all last winter, then in March, when there was a black slush all over the streets, we broke up. She didn't want me touching her anymore. She said that if I could keep my hands off her, she'd think about seeing me again. But my hands were always cold, and I couldn't help slipping them up under her sweater and just cupping them there until I forgot how cold I was. But that was a long time ago.

When Primo and Tony are finished, Dominic and I have maybe two tons of hindquarters and sirloins and sides to hang. The cooler's foggy with our breath, but underneath our clothes and two aprons, we're sweating. Then our hands start to cramp, and when we're heaving a quarter up to the hook sometimes it slips and comes down on our our shins or our feet. It gets sawdust all over it, and we've got to wipe it off with a rag, and that only makes the cold worse.

That sawdust. It comes in big burlap bags. A guy named Wilbur brings it in once a week in a pickup truck. He's from out in the boondocks somewhere, out there on the ridges back of the river where there's a sawmill and people still keep pigs and chickens. We haul the bags off the truck and roll them down the basement steps. There's one light bulb, back in the corner, and we heave the bags against the wall that smells like the river. Wood chips and sawdust and the river. Sometimes we have a smoke down there, but it's dangerous. If the boss caught us we'd be fired on the spot. But it's warm, and the smells are like camping.

After we've got the meat hung and all the boxes stacked, it's time to start pulling the cases. Four-thirty, a day of cold and complaining, and you've got to finish up with reaching in and pulling the trays out, slapping a piece of paper over the steaks and chops and city chicken, and then stacking them in the cooler. And wait on customers, too. And when that's done, you start on the chickens. There's maybe fifty of them in the case, stiff and numb in ice. You drag them out of there, the sharp crushed ice jabbing your hands, and you drop the chickens in a box and lug them back. But there's always some customer who wants one, right in the middle of your job. "Let me see that one," she says, pointing at some measly carcass clear down in the front of the case. You reach way in and pull it out, your hands so numb you can hardly grab it, and you lift it up over the top of the counter so she can eyeball it. "Too big," she says. "Find me a smaller one." That goes on two or three times, and finally she says, "Well, I don't know. None of them looks any good to me. I'll come back tomorrow," and she leaves.

Then it's quitting time. The boss locks the front doors and Violet, the cashier, hunches over the day's receipts and the register chatters and rings for another half hour. In the back room, the women crowd the john, changing their clothes and smoking cigarettes. Sometimes I hang around, leaning against the frame of the door between the front and the back, watching Violet out there, busy, humming some Serbian tune to herself, the green lamp in the cashier's cage like a light way down in the river, deep down, deep and quiet. Then I go back. Primo and Tony sit on one of the big tables, their bloody aprons folded across their laps. They make wisecracks as the rest of us haul the last trash out to the dumpster.

"That all the faster you can go, Dominic?" Tony says. "You got polio or what?"

Primo shakes his head. "Hey, Dominic," he yells, "You breakin em, man."

Dominic and I stand by the sink later, having a smoke.

"Fucking job," Dominic says. His hands are raw, frozen half the day from the cold, scalded the other half from washing the trays. "Fucking Primo and Tony."

"Yeah," I say.

But all the time I'm tuning it out, like the tiredness lets me do. I'm tuning it all out, the meaning of it, so that the words people say are just noise, a kind of music. All day's becoming a song, snow falling out of the gray sky outside, millsmoke and snow, the hard faces and dark clothes of the customers, the red blood of the cutting blocks pooling and dripping, the aching in my knees. "Goddama, you breakin em," *la la la*. "You sumbitch," *do se do*. All day's a song. "You breakin em, breakin em. You breakin em."

Yeah.

The Dance

Her name was Effie Morel. She was one of the most popular girls in the senior class, and second only in voluptuousness to Nutsi Campagna, an olive-skinned brunette as lush as Sophia Loren. Effie was cute, smooth-skinned, with an upturned nose and a body tending to a flushed, moist fullness: just ripe.

It was the weekly K of C dance. The boys stood at a scruffy parade rest on one side of the floor while the girls chatted in random squads on the other. That night Effie wore a cashmere sweater, a blue straight skirt and black pumps as shiny as anthracite. Backroom consensus was that she had the finest legs in town.

I was governed mainly by hormones at the time, and by my secret, often agonizing desires. As a result, girls were stimuli to wild confusions, disorderly excitements. I had not civilized myself enough, nor had school nor time nor experience tamed me sufficiently for me to behave calmly, reasonably. Even nature herself had stacked the deck against me and other boys in my class: the girls were more mature, more contained than we were, much less liable to the sudden flarings of self-consciousness that vaporized our common sense. Often, we were goofy, and we knew it. Worst of all, we couldn't help it.

I free-floated at those dances. My first love had moved away during my sophomore year; I had not cultivated any serious romance since. I had befriended many girls, but passion was not an element in our relationships. On the mornings of those Saturday evening dances, I played sandlot football recklessly, scrimmaging until my object-less desire grew blunt with fatigue.

When the DJ announced the first Lady's Choice, Effie walked over to me. Would you like to dance? I most certainly would. Her right arm rose over my shoulder, then settled warmly. She pulled me close to her. Close close.

We danced, slowly, across the floor, her body pressing mine like a rush of humid tropical air. What's going on? I thought. What is this? When the music ended, she smiled up at me, and I saw, to one side, Jimmy Fiti, the quarterback of the football team and Effie's boyfriend since the beginning of junior year. He stared.

I retreated to the refreshment room for a smoke. Fiti came in a few minutes later. For all his athletic achievement, he was a quiet, almost withdrawn kid. Though we had been teammates a couple of times during high school we were not friends. And there was a greater distance between us, too: Fiti was capable of violence, quickly, remorselessly. I had seen him transformed from a silent bystander into a demon, loosing a fury of punches on the South End bus one morning. Guys still talked of the mauling he gave Dominic Ciccone that day.

"Why you dancing with Effie?" Fiti said.

"Lady's Choice," I said. "She asked me."

Fiti shook his arms. His and Effie's was a universally known and unchallenged attachment. I saw anger and bewilderment in his eyes, but he turned away and went back into the dance. I finished my cigarette, settled myself down, and followed a little later.

For a time I stood leaning against one of the mirrored walls, watching the girls fast dance with each other. Few guys did the Jerk or Pony or the Mashed Potatoes; these were considered acceptable only for girls. I do not know what they thought, those almost-women, as we watched them out there in the lights, but to me they seemed caught up in a rapture of oblivion; they seemed in a frenzied heaven of their own, and we boys in the shadows simply did not exist for them. Girls, many of us suspected, were another kind of being altogether, and though we were dreadfully and awkwardly attracted, I think we feared them, feared their self-contained mystery, their flushed and unaccountable temptation of us out on the dance floor. And we feared, most powerfully, the realization that what they did was not for our amusement at all, but for some strange, unfathomable reason of their own. I do not think we would have been much surprised if, at the end of the song, they had all cried out at once, together, and then vanished, never to return, only the fading scents of their perfume and delicate sweat lingering behind for us boys, stunned and forsaken, to remember them by.

Effie was among the Bacchantes out there on the floor. Fiti stood against the wall opposite me, a couple of his heavy cousins to one side, alternately glaring at me and watching Effie dance. When the music ended the DJ announced that he'd slow it down now, and Roy Orbison's *Crying* wailed from the speakers. I watched Fiti edge his way through a clutch of girls and touch Effie on the shoulder. I

saw her turn sharply away from him. I saw him standing there,
his feet concrete on the floor, his face motionless, grim.

Soon the DJ called another Lady's Choice. Effie made her way
among the girls and glided toward me once more. Dread mingled
with excitement; I grew dizzy for a second.

Would you like to dance?

Forever, I thought. Always.

Again she pressed herself against me, her hand cupping mine
closely to her breast. I could feel her heartbeat, I could feel her motion, her breathing, the dancing flowing upward through her body
and into my arms. When the music stopped, she did not pull away,
but remained close to me, supple and relaxed, her head resting on
my shoulder.

I opened my eyes. Fiti stood a few feet before us, arms folded
across his chest. One of his cousins leaned over and whispered something to him. His eyes fixed on mine. Effie stiffened: she saw him.
She pressed herself even more closely to me, the heat, the valleys
and softnesses of her. And suddenly I knew what was happening.
I tried to step back from her, but she clutched at me, and there was
no passion in her grasp, but something else, something angry and
bitter and despairing. All within me chilled; I jerked away. Fiti leaped
toward me. Effie stepped in front of him, hands on his chest. "No!"
she cried.

I found myself, I do not know how long after, in the refreshments room again. From the alcove where the girl's restroom was,
I could hear laughter and talking. When the door opened, a warm
exhalation issued from it, smelling of hair spray and perfume. People
passed by, singly, in pairs, in long loose groups. But I was alone
through it all. My friends must have stopped to speak with me, but
I was unaware, tense with the danger and excitement of what had
happened. Even the energy of the dance and the crowd could not
displace my fear.

The dance ended. I stayed in the refreshments room until the
voices faded as people walked down the long straight stairs to the
lobby at the bottom. I grabbed my jacket from the coat room at one
side of the stairway and started down. There were Effie and Fiti,
face-to-face about two thirds of the way down. I watched as Effie
sneered at Fiti's attempts to understand her; she laughed a miserable, too-high laugh when he grabbed her wrists and shouted, 'Listen! Look at me!'

I felt invisible, unbodied—dead, in a way. Though intimately involved in their argument, I had no place in it really. Not to Effie especially. As I listened, her motives became clear. Fiti hadn't paid her the attention she'd wanted, he'd done something she didn't like, she had used me to get back at him. She had lied with her flesh, her eyes, with her soft moist hands that curved against the back of my neck as we danced. The realization of that lie, the meaning of it, shook me again. I steadied myself on the handrail.

They went down at last, still shouting at one another, pathetically holding hands. I lingered on the stairs, giving them plenty of time to be gone. Then I went down myself. I pushed the glass door open into a bitter night, gray ice glinting in patches on the sidewalk. It was the same world I had walked inside from just a few hours before, and yet it wasn't. Not the same world at all. I walked south, passing the greasy exhaust of the Arcade Grill, my shoes loud over the steel cellar doors in the sidewalk. A stern wind raked at my face. Overhead, a few stars glared in the building-crowded sky, their light sharp as the points of ice picks.

Old Woman River

Water
1

I can only deeply think near water,
where the cold-blooded fish
steer in a constant current, contained
and sufficient as air,
who don't know me and don't care.

But the long grief is contracted,
illness that it is, that drives me
drinking until dawn, reckless
on the low roads as the sun blasts me from
the east,
only close to rivers, in the company of
glitterings
and shimmerings
of the things below.

2

Always when I slow, grow still,
then I think of her arising,
steadily from streaming trash and floodbits,
flotsam of the farm,
effluvia of all the efforts of the city
to remain,
bromo bottles, sogged softballs,
the bloated guts of dogs,
rags and plastic bags with stuff like brains
in them,
the stems of pipes, pockets,
gnawed hocks of ham,
knuckles nibbled to a shine like dice,
and sickness lays me low.

3

So beneath the willows or the trestle see me,
slipping slowly as the river calls, then falls away.
The water's many edges, thinly beaten gold,
want to take me, bit by infinite bit,
away from the dark bog of the shore,
not screaming, silent as a depth of stone,
from the heron's spear-ground and discarded bone,
to where she waits, transparent as the rain,
and we can be alone.

(c. 1972)

I had just turned fourteen when for the first time in my life someone of my age and acquaintance died. Her name could have come right out of a James Joyce novel; her manner of death, drowning in the river, could have made her into Anna Livia Plurabelle. But no such transformations took place. Jackie Finnegan, age thirteen, fourteen, resident of the South End of Steubenville, Ohio, drowned to death, having been pitched suddenly overboard from a boat into the Ohio River. Her body had lodged beneath the surface for a couple of days before the draggers snagged it with grappling hooks and hauled it ashore. For the first and only time in my life, I skipped school, and haunted the riverbanks in dread, watching and listening as the searchers labored in fog and heat.

It was eight or nine years later, as far as I can recall, that I first tried to write about it. At the time I was immersed in the history of Steubenville, grabbling its depths and darknesses, and it appears that somehow her death had without my awareness become lodged deeply in the story of my place.

If only she had died in Joyce's book, she might have been able to flow into life again, walking up out of the river. Like James Wright's miraculous women in *Shall We Gather At The River*, resurrected across the river from Bridgeport, Ohio, she might have risen to dry her wings and go on to her freshman year in high school. I might then have been able to catch up with her again. If the death she suffered in the river had been purely literary or mythic, anything could have happened.

She could have grown up to be even more beautiful than my memory of her. Every day, while watching me do fancy dives from the high board at Beatty Park pool, she sat combing her brass-red hair, so long that it flowed out across the bleachers from her sides like pools of melted pennies. I knew she was watching me; she knew I knew. One of my friends from the public school had told her that I liked her, and though she never spoke to me directly, though I never even heard her voice, we were connected in some spiritual way that would not admit of communication by anything so common as words.

It is now more than thirty years since the day she died. One marriage has long ago broken and blown away and now I am trying to be worthy of another. I have two children, boys, the oldest of them just a year or so younger than Jackie Finnegan was when she died, and I live 250 miles from where that death occurred. I have a busy, sometimes hectic and disorderly life, the usual chronic misgivings about the conduct of my affairs, many responsibilities in several arenas. Why then, with all of this to occupy my attention, do I return to the death of this girl, to whom I never spoke a word in my life?

And return to that death I do. A few years ago, for what I thought to be purely literary reasons, I compiled an informal list of all the attempts I had made over the years to come to terms with her passing, to put her to rest in my memory. "Like looking for something you don't want to find," a note I scribbled at the head of it says. Several stories, a half-dozen poems, passages in several essays, and even the substitution of her for the central figure in my re-tellings of such urban folklore as The Vanishing Hitchhiker, were attempts to figure her death out, to say it once and for all; to finish it, if I could. But at last I have realized that her death has come to occupy a place in me more permanent and more inaccessible than grief. I no longer feel sorrow in remembering her; she is like an island, dim and a bit uncertain of outline in dawn light and fog, out in the middle of the river of mind. Going somewhere else in the reaches of thought and memory, I occasionally travel past her, feeling her presence as one feels the presence, in fog, of an indistinct but familiar sandbar or snag. Her death is a part of the riverscape of my mind.

Off The Papermill

I am tasking my once-
lighter body
with loves it must have

died to,
wishing its aging weight
higher than its dreams
might go.
All my young, impeccable miles
file beneath me,
a river of visions,
for there is myself, on a
raft of crates,
calling all the
lost daughters
of friends.
When their answer sends
itself, a thin silt
ascending, so does water,
washing me down
into times deeper than I know.

How can my flesh
be so dangerous, to drown
and revive
me again, knowing their
names, their ages?

(c. 1968)

In his book *Self Interviews*, James Dickey writes, "I think a river is the most beautiful thing in nature. Any river. Some are more beautiful than others, but any river is more beautiful than anything else I know."

The river of my grandfather and father, the river of my own boyish romanticism and nostalgia, was indeed a beautiful thing. Perhaps the river retained so long its innocent beauty for me because however intensely wandering my boyhood had been, I had never once been in a boat anywhere on it. This is a strange fact, given the long history of hand-built boats in my family and the unstintingly riparian character of the culture my Irish forebears built along the Ohio shore. Papers my father sent me while I was working on our family history include drawings of two shantyboats occupied by family and friends. One, a stubby, rather top-heavy vessel labeled in my father's neat blueprint lettering, "Jess Dray's

House Boat," sports two windows to a side, one at either end, and an old-fashioned metal stovepipe coming up out of the exact center of its roof. The other appears under this notation: "James Scanlon and Cal Greer's house boats resembled this." James Scanlon was my great-grandmother's uncle or brother—who for some reason preferred life on the river to living in a house. Perhaps it's because his shantyboat was the deluxe model, with porches at either end, so he could go a-fishing upstream or down.

But I never got off shore, except to wade a foot or two out to retrieve a stringer of catfish that had croaked and struggled into deeper water. I had never sat down in a boat and felt underneath me, and at the ends of its oars, the river's deep power and flow, its brown inevitable force.

Nor had I felt its nameless cold, experienced the darkness of its wreck-strewn bottom, blindly nudged the inert pallor of the blank-eyed six-foot catfish lurking in its depths, nor felt press in upon me the inescapable suck and pressure of the death it bore within itself.

And that's strange too, because it's not that I had never heard of its destructive side. I still remember vividly my grandfather telling me about the 1936 flood, and how the next door neighbors—this while pointing just across the side yard to the very exits he would mention—had to evacuate by climbing into boats from their upstairs windows. And every day I visited there, I stopped and leaned over to see the notch he and my father had cut into the curb in front of their house at 118 Logan St. to mark the high water then.

And I could smell something of the river's danger in the mold in the coal cellar and fruit cellar there, as I would later smell it even further away from the river, in the basement of the Junedale Meat Market clear up on South Fourth Street when I would be sent down by the boss to bring up a sack of sawdust to strew across the greasy wooden floors.

But I must not have believed it then. Young, only driftingly and sporadically conscious of mortality, chance, impermanence, I simply ignored it. And then Jackie Finnegan drowned.

In my early twenties, my master's thesis consisted of a series of poems chronicling the public and private history of Steubenville. It was my first attempt to make some sense out of where I came from, and how my origins shaped who I was. One of the poems remembers the Ohio Theater, a dilapidated establishment on Market Street when I was very young, and which must have been, in Steubenville's Little Chicago days, a burlesque house. The poem imagines a stripper from there, lately retired, wanting to cleanse herself of her past by plunging into the river, and being born anew. I see now that, along with the drowned girl of "Water," she is among the first of many avatars of Jackie Finnegan, and that her monologue fuses several aspects of the girl, the woman, the temptress, and the goddess.

A Stripper, Lately Retired From The Ohio Theater, Contemplates The River At Steubenville

Unclothed by ten long days
of August, almost forgetting
hog-call, gab and cackle,
rows on rows of eyes,
I want to spill myself from sequins
into sand and hand
this body down.

On the river, bubbles gem up bright
from rocks and rotten wood,
and burst in daylight free
of teasing exits. I've bumped and ground
in public in this cocky town,
can go no further than the peace
of wading in, to the snorts and brays
of miners hunchbacked on the shore.

I would like to glide down
through the willows and the reeds
and launch myself, unseen,
some legend at the outset,
to float face up beneath the bridges
so they could see me only as I passed,
then drift in shallows bare of eyes,
womanly, unknown, till they'd fish me in
with nets or lines like some important relic
and fire the courthouse cannon
for the first time in a hundred years.

But no: the moth in me is tired
of lights, flames, bloodshot eyes:
I want to make the bankers long thought dead
revive from catfish graves and kiss me,
keeping me for stories when it's dark,
I want to drift alive in inlets
when the moon's up over boys
who fish for carp, and be their mothers,
not asleep at home,
but diving with them, gracefully and naked
in the sinkholes,
searching with them for their wedding rings
of stone, their wives of
rainwash, young and clean and
waiting, singing secretly within
them like a thousand tiny frogs;
I want to lie with them
at sunrise on the shore,
and to hold, at last, their fine unbroken
bodies in my arms.

(c. 1970-71)

O Jesus, Mary, and Joseph! (as my great-aunties Madigan all
five of them would have said) help us to understand these women,
these sisters and daughters, these beloveds and departeds, these
mothers and grannies and wives. Help us brothers and sons and
lovers and fathers to understand ourselves with them. What are we
to make of them and ourselves and our lives with and among them?

The baddest guy I knew in Steubenville was a skinny punk
with loose sallow skin and a sullen attitude who apparently had so
little joy in his days that he would regularly beat up on kids as if it
were their fault that his life was so bleak.

Afterwards, watching him as he sat red-faced and alone, shivering in the green vinyl of the bus seat, I never got the sense that he
was any happier for having kicked some ass. Rather I got the sense
that there was something else he wanted, something more or different than blood. He hunched there muttering to himself, sucking
his own skinned knuckles, and sometimes, despite himself, he cried.

Nevertheless, this fellow, as we were accustomed to saying,
was bad. That didn't mean in the late 50's and early 60's milltown

working class times anything like wicked or evil. Wickedness certainly wasn't this fellow's problem; even as children we knew something was wrong with him; some dis-ease, some blight, or bleakness, of the same horrid color as the acid-spoiled creeks that spilled from the strip mines and on down through backyards all around us, had gathered in his heart, and every once in a while overflowed its banks. Wickedness was much more subtle; wickedness was trickery and deceit and betrayal and mortal sin; wickedness was the witch on the bike in *The Wizard of Oz*, or the stepsisters in *Cinderella*, or the crucifixion of Jesus on Golgotha. Wicked was what Mary Magdalene had been, but then was no more, because of Jesus. True wickedness, we knew, happened only rarely, and mostly among adults.

So bad, in the parlance of the day, meant nasty, physically intimidating, aggressive. Also, by curious extension, it could also mean beautiful or admirable, as in that's a bad motorcycle, or he's a bad runner. If a fellow in a fist fight back of school took a number of punches to the face, but never yielded to tears, and at last clipped crimson and opened the lip of his opponent with a curt jab, then he was bad. If a boy did a two-and-a-half gainor off the high board at Beatty Park and wiped out so that he landed full on his back, but climbed out of the water grinning, he was bad. A bad car was fast, powerful, beautifully customized.

So of the truly bad—the wicked—we boys were, officially and publicly, at least, completely innocent. There was a time for a couple of crucial years right after puberty when we warned each other endlessly, in a state of dreadful fascination, about "homos" and when we thought we saw them everywhere, and almost stopped hitchhiking entirely so as to avoid being confronted (we had plans worked out with or without umbrellas or sticks or knives to fend off attacks.)

But I wouldn't have known how to be bad in the darkest sense of the word, nor would I have had much opportunity in my boyhood. Steubenville was a small town even smaller than it seemed to me back then, when an auntie or uncle or cousin or neighbor, or even your own mother of father, might show up anytime, anywhere, and eyeball you and take in the whole scene.

It was smaller even than that careful snoopiness, that almost universal supervision. For example, maybe there were whorehouses still in Steubenville, but all we heard were rumors. That part of the city's story was in the distant past, or at least that's what we boys were led to believe.

In my junior year of high school though, the local Key Club, of which I was the most minor of minor members, took over the city government for a day. I am sure the ruling fathers intended this to be an education and inspiration; the boys who were mayor and judge and police chief must have tasted something of the power of their offices. But for me, the day unfolded idly in the basement of the Court House, where, ensconced as Clerk of Courts, I spent a solitary day with a dozen file cabinets stuffed with the flood-stained, dog-eared arrest records and mug shots of what seemed an entire generation of women. I remember none of them individually, though their faces collectively I recall as either lean and sad-eyed, or squintingly bloated, as if recently beaten. And their hats—they all wore hats, decades of hats, historical periods of hats, ecstasies and elegies of hats, each of them shabby, slightly off-center or out of shape: the hats of sluts and floozies.

Now there is the beginning of some wickedness. Not in these prostitutes, their hats, nor their sins, whatever and if ever they might have been, but in my quick characterization of them as sluts or floozies. Some may well have been brazen sensualists and immoralists; but knowing the town, the mills, the region, I am pretty sure that many were simple women down on their luck, mothers some of them, widowed by the mill or railroad or coal mine, trying to make it in a world of hard men, hard jobs, hard times.

I remember being suddenly struck, down there in that river-damp darkness, with a strange anxiety. What if in my snooping among those records of the past, I encountered my own grandmother, or one of my rosary-toting aunties? I would have been frozen with shock, arrested in a calamity of curiosity and new knowledge, my heart fluttering, my mouth forming its first great No.

The face and form of her would become clear, coalescing out of the hundreds of photographs and names. A kind of Shadow Grandmother would arise in my mind, some archetypal Old Woman. And I would have to imagine her, reconstruct her in my mind, and reconstruct the men she had been with, the litany of their names, the smells of oil and coal dust and printer's ink and gasoline and carp and shad on their hands and then imagine seeing her, many years later, on that bus with the wild fighting boy. She steps back from where she was sitting, comes my way, and for a moment I expect she will comfort and shelter me, offer some boon of insight and calm. But she passes on and embraces as if some lost prodigal that bloody-knuckled suffering punk, and smoothes his greasy hair, and yes, even kisses him, saying It's all right. It'll all be fine. It's okay.

Don't we all have something like this Shadow Grandmother, an ancestress beaten but undefeated by life? A survivor, smelling of whiskey and soap, blood and cheap toilet-water? There's a photo from the Ulster Museum in Ireland, reprinted in a recent issue of *Humanities* magazine. It has entered me, this old image, as fully and completely as the diary of my great-grandmother, if I were by some incredible and undeserved grace to stumble upon such a thing. Two women (it is difficult to tell how old, or young, they are — the caption reads only *Girls Working In A Potato Field*), two women, then, work the hills of a potato field somewhere in Ireland. They labor at the bottom of a rise of land; the field's crest towers over them, foreshortened by the lens. The one to the right stands with her back almost completely to the camera. In the gray shadowless light, her shoulder blades are visible beneath her dark dress, and her right arm is drawn back, guiding her spade. Below her and to the left stands the other, in a black dress and shawl, captured in mid-motion as she lifts her spade from the row.

I know that work. My own flesh has inherited the rhythm of spade and earth. I can feel the cold wind on my cheek as surely as those women had felt it; I can smell the mold and earth at my feet, hear the rooks calling over the far hills, smell the bittersweet smoke of the peat fire back in their damp cottage.

And in this knowledge it is as if I am giving birth, painlessly, in a dream, to myself. I am watching the women who were my mothers, and the deja vu attending my viewing of this photo, and of the mug shots of the Steubenville women, and the voice that entered me when I was writing about the stripper at the Ohio Theater — these are all more holes in time, pits through which I fall into the past and its sometimes dreadful knowledge.

No wonder the boy on the bus had to weep. Though he fought with matter and with time, the incorrigible present, the relentless and uncontrollable incarnating of the now, he could not overcome and control it. I see that he wept for himself, trapped in the same one-way plunge into time and death that we are all trapped in, and

I see that he was, perhaps without knowing it, haunted by some formless and unarticulated notion of perfection, some gentle, fulsome, nurturing Mother Country he could never recover or achieve. I see now that had I ever gotten into a boat in my youth, I might never have been able to fight back up the current, into the past; I would have been, as many are these days, lost to myself, adrift on the continual birth of Change, seeing only downstream. It is memory which keeps us from becoming lost, washed down river, and that protects us from the predatory one-way of time's arrow. Because of some unnamed trauma, perhaps because of some imperfection of nerve or flesh, that boy on the bus had forgotten everything. And so he pummeled the Here and Now, hoping hopelessly in bloody anger, grief, and loss to immobilize and defeat it. The poor sucker didn't know what he was doing.

It's an old story. I am reminded of my friend Larry Smith's essay "The Company of Widows," which appears in his collection of prose entitled *Beyond Rust*. I think of its punning title, referring not only to his mother and the friends she kept company with, but to the Steubenville and Mingo Junction, Ohio steel mills and related companies that wore out, then abandoned their husbands. The writer recalls a conversation with a city planner in Steubenville, who, depressed over the displacement caused by dubious urban renewal, left Smith with a phrase that haunted him: "Abandonment creates its own culture." One of the hallmarks of that culture, the planner said, was that people trapped in it live unconnected, using up the present.

Using up the present.

It's what the mills did, the big corporations that funneled the profits from them into whatever black holes of power and wealth and tawdry achievement such industrial capitalist booty disappears. They did not try to imagine and plan for a better future, nor for a healthier environment beyond that mandated by laws passed hundreds of miles away, distant from the local community and its intricate and unique local problems, nor did they acknowledge the lessons of the past as recent as the Dust Bowl, lessons that might have warned them that we cannot consume the resources and health and landscape of a place and a people with impunity: there will be consequences. No wonder their own workers, surrounded by such a culture, used up the present. When the mills failed, as was inevitable, when so many company men milled around in abandonment, there was little else for them, spiritually or psychologically, to use. And their wives? Their wives sometimes became what they used up, too.

And it was the river that brought this culture to the Valley, the river that opened the way into these hills dense, blessed, and cursed with coal, their hollows and coves crudely sutured by railroads sidings and lines to the mines, then later patchworked with innumerable zigzag wounds, like some Frankenstein's monster of a landscape, all the stitches ending or beginning at the mills and slag heaps and scrap iron yards.

It was the river that brought my own ancestors, Margaret Cavanaugh among the earliest, who came by ship from Ireland, then over the mountains and down the river to Steubenville, and whose family name my oldest son bears. It was the river that gave forth its plentiful fish to me in boyhood, that glinted and flashed in the twilight all summer, that seemed a haven of healing silence within its willow-fringed haunts. It was the river that rose brown and violent and heedless and cold in the spring floods among the cottonwoods and across the railroad tracks, leaving dead carp and strangled catfish and the debris of forest, farm, and town tangled and stinking on the ballast and ties. "La Belle Riviere," the French called it, "the beautiful river."

It was this river—bountiful mother, haggard crone, victim, victimizer, comforter, mystery, brute lesson—that took and held Jackie Finnegan, and still holds her, she whom I never held.

PART TWO

Mike Swartz's Winter 1957-1958 coon catch; L to R:
Danny Reed, Richard Hague, Roger Swartz, dogs Tubby and Chubby
(Hague family photo)

Mowing the Bald

One

To my family for the past quarter of a century, it has always been the "Farm." Actually, the place is no more a farm than a wolf is a house pet. Situated a couple of miles east of Graysville, Ohio down County Road 12, a roller coaster gravel bed of switch backs, overhanging brush, and soft-shouldered curves, the Farm is one of the highest spots in Monroe County. Monroe, in turn, is one of the hilliest counties in Appalachian Ohio. Less than a mile down Greenbrier, as the ridge is known, a Geodesic Survey benchmark identifies Master's Knob as the champion of altitude in these parts; the Farm misses by about the height of a good barn.

I first set foot on the place in November, 1960. I was thirteen. A photo from that visit survives; there's not much to see beyond the skinny figure of a boy with his hands deep in his coat pockets. If the face reveals anything, it's a mixture of alienation and physical discomfort. "I'm here," it suggests, "and I'm cold, and I want to go home." Distanced from that boy who was myself, I feel sympathy. There's something of the displaced person in his look. Greenbrier did indeed seem like a foreign land in those days. Where I'd grown up in Steubenville, its thirty thousand inhabitants, the bustle and noise of the mills, the regular and strangely calming drone of coal trucks through the night, had made me something of a town person. My forays into the woods and the scrub growth struggling to reclaim an old strip mine near where I lived had in part prepared me for such a landscape as the Farm's, but not completely. I'd never experienced such silence, for example, nor had I been able to see as far as I could down there. Ohio's Seven Ranges — the first surveyed lands of the Northwest Territory — washboarded off in the distance, and from the knob overlooking the road, I could see a light in Lewisville, nearly ten road miles away, glowing like a stalled planet over Foreaker Meadow at night. At first, the place frightened me. Its scant human population, its raw natural features, its distance from home — all of this alarmed me. Going there was a chore, an ordeal.

In the summer of 1962, my father began regular trips to the Farm, and I was his surly tagalong. We owned a 1960 Chevrolet station wagon, a pale green model the color of a young katydid. Its back seat folded down—I mention this because we slept in the wagon for the years before we bought a trailer—and I got to know every hinge and every seam of that seat through endless claustrophobic nights. The wagon's interior reeked of gasoline fumes, for we'd begun hauling the mower down. That was, oddly enough, the beginning of the Farm's comeback.

"The place was barren," my father remembers. "Mostly sumac and dust. There wasn't even any sassafras growing on it in those days, and sassafras'll grow anywhere." I remember mostly the heat and the rocky hardness of the ground. I don't know if it had ever been farmed.

But surely it had been logged, as all of the county had been, and most of the trees in the woods, save for a few wild hickories and fenceline beeches, were scrub growth persimmon, quaking aspen, and pioneer tulip poplars, interspersed with remnant stands of maples, oaks, black walnuts, and gnarled pitch pines. Most of the soil up the hill from where we stayed had long ago been washed far down into Brown's Run.

Still, my father began to mow. Into the silence would roar the voice of the engine. This would be followed immediately by dervishes of dust, whirling tornadoes that drew up into their columns a moil of grit and weedbits and small stones. My father looked like a man pushing a storm.

Slowly but surely, though, mowing and applications of lime brought what had been a dusty bald thatched sparsely with broom sedge back to a richer, more diverse soil-making greenness. After a few years, the shade of the established growth allowed other plants to take hold, and eventually a lawn of clover and rye grass grew to the rocky edge of the roadcut, where butterfly weed bloomed orange in the sun. A struggling wild cherry began to fill out, and a stand of sumacs thrived at the edge of the gully washing down to Brown's Run, and was joined soon by a clutch of sassafras seedlings. Most of this would have happened without our interference, we knew, but the recovery seemed somehow as much for our benefit as for the place's, a kind of benediction.

We planted other trees, too. The first were twelve hundred white pines my father ordered from the Soil Bank Program. We set them out during the spring of 1963, my father in one row, my brother and I in another, and Ed Daugherty, a neighbor boy, in a third. Recalling that work, I think of Millet's painting of women laboring in a field. The figures capture the hardness of the work, but also its peasant strength and dignity. Never to have planted, never to have stretched and bent over the earth in working for the future, is to have missed something elemental, important. Planting trees is planting dreams.

I was beginning to be changed by the Farm. My initial discomfort ripened into acceptance; going down there lost its strangeness, and I began to feel attached to the place. I liked to walk back into the pine grove in successive years, measuring the new season's growth, listening to the wind through the thickening needles. I think the fact that the pines grew so well without tending impressed me; I learned the toughness of nature, the simple achievement that life can accomplish so gracefully on its own. Little of that was fully clear to me then, of course. I was Wordsworth's "glad animal" at the time, a being mostly of sensation, a devotee of the physical, not the philosophical. Still, I learned from the greening bald and the climbing pines. We planted more trees, a few at a time, in later years. Russian olives, Chinese chestnuts, even a few peach trees. The olives and chestnuts have done well, but the peach trees, though set on the south slope in the lee of the hill, have always struggled. They're past their prime now, and have made fruit in only a handful of seasons. They're stunted, their tops weakened by insects and hammered by storms, but they have an antique durability to them, a patient endurance that recalls bristlecone pines.

Though my father and I gradually took to the place almost like natives, sinking the roots of association and care deep into its rocky hollows and recovering woods, knowing just where to find the stand of mayapples, or the dead walnut worked by a pileated woodpecker, or the tiny spring whose source was the stony darkness at the base of twin hickories far over the eastern hillside, my mother was never really comfortable at the Farm; she still isn't. In the early Sixties, we hauled a trailer, a thirty-footer, the ninety miles from Empire, Ohio, where we bought it, down to the Farm and installed it atop the bald, its stern abutting a tough crab apple that had sprung up there. One of the first things we did, after picking up the cabinet doors that had been thrown from their hinges during the crazy drive down, was to build a back stoop. My archetypal experience of solar energy occurred on that stoop: the reflective skin of the trailer behind me, I sat facing the sun one cool, clear, and windless June day, and without sweating or discomfort, felt the sunlight literally warm my bones. My spirit, kindling in that heat, rose to a prompt and lasting happiness that carried me ballooning through the season like a young spider on its filament.

There were bookcases in that trailer, built into its bow, so to speak, under the curving windows at its hitch end. These we stocked quickly: old Boy Scout manuals, bulletins from the Government Printing Office, second-hand collections of nature essays, back issues of *National Geographics*. Once, my mother pulled a copy of *Moby Dick* from the shelf, and along with it came a blacksnake, all four feet of it, calmly over the back of the couch and across her lap. Though she hung curtains and installed rugs and vacuumed with a vengeance, she never fully domesticated the trailer. The snakes are permanent, their gunmetal coils the signature of the true owner of the place.

During those high school years, I got to know the Farm in various weathers and in the most subtle modulations of light and dark. Summer thunderstorms were often violent on that exposed knob; once, in a great wind, the trailer was blown off its foundation. My father came to find it listing to the starboard like a foundering ship, and his buddies on the line gang of the telephone company helped him re-set it.

A decade later, just after the two summers I'd spent there alone, a lightning bolt struck the new well housing, blowing the head off it and destroying the pump controls. Light bulbs inside the trailer burst. At about the same time, I sat out Hurricane Agnes there, through two days of rain and wind, my dog cowering under the kitchen table, the garden over the hill transformed into twin clay-yellow ponds.

Storms like those leave their marks on the land: there are still the wrecks of trees blown over by Agnes lying across the gully leading down to Brown's Run, and there are strangely abbreviated pines here and there along Greenbrier, their tops shattered by winds or by the snows that burdened them during the blizzard years of the late Seventies. Such events leave marks on the spirits of those humans present during them, too. If ever you have succumbed to sentimentalism in your relationship to Nature, such violence draws you up short, and quickly. The bridges to false calm are washed out. You must wrestle, like Jacob with the angel, and acknowledge the strength of fear.

There were less dramatic but equally instructive hints of nature's darkness down there as well. In the early days, we almost always saw copperheads on the road between Graysville and the Farm. They fascinated and thrilled me, and their presence made of me a careful walker in the woods. I learned never to step blindly over a log: I looked first, sometimes even poking with the stick I carried. On stony hillsides, I traveled slowly but noisily, flushing any lurking copperheads or rattlers out before me. I didn't have an irrational fear of snakes, just a healthy respect for them. I'd kept snakes as a hobby all during my boyhood, and knew something of their ways. It was the other, smaller animals, that gave me the most trouble.

When we first began to go to the Farm, my father and I would stop at Whitacre's, the general store for those parts, to chew the fat and catch up on the local news. Mr. Whitacre once kept a groundhog as a pet. He'd trained it to respond to his whistle, which he demonstrated one afternoon. It would waddle out from its den beneath his back stoop, lumber across the lawn of the homestead and across the gravel lot in front of the store. Then, ascending the porch steps as awkwardly as a seal out of water, it would affectionately gnaw at the leather of his shoes.

For all its genius, I'm sure that groundhog, as all other pedestrians in the county, was nevertheless plagued by ticks. I've seen ticks the size of ripe catawba grapes hanging from the jowls of worn-out beagles. I've seen ticks lodged on the very eyelids of mutts that scraped and scraped at them, but uselessly; I've awakened at night to feel them exploring the hair at the nape of my neck, and by the time I've pulled myself up from nightmare into the real dark, have discovered their tenacious hold. Once, near-delirious with disgust, I wedged the blade of my knife between my scalp and a tick, and beheaded the little bugger. This was dangerous therapy, for the tick can carry Rocky Mountain Spotted Fever and the strange Lyme Disease, among who knows what other maladies. It is imperative to remove the infecting mouthparts. The common method is an application of nail polish remover to the beast, which causes it to back out, withdrawing its piercing and sucking apparatus. But I was a bachelor at the time, living almost as wildly as a feral cat, and that particular item was not one I kept in stock. Nor could I work myself up to the legendary health of one fellow I had heard about down there, a man who could cuss so profoundly, so therapeutically, it was said, that "a tick'd peel off him quick as the skin off a hammered finger."

Time after time down there in those early days, such comic disarmaments of troubles had their effect on me: the beauties, wonders, and providences of the woods and hills and in the talk of the people there strengthened and revived me. I grew less serious, less hassled by things, knowing that there were gags and tales that would lighten any moment, and that could transform the worry of life into opportunities for laughter and growth. A good thing, too. For the second part of my life at the Farm, commencing with the decade following college, was a rough one. To this day I am convinced that the Farm saved my life.

Two

In Saul Bellows' *Henderson The Rain King*, the central character, a struggling pilgrim named Gene Henderson, embarks on an African journey in answer to a voice inside him which cries "I want, I want." Henderson has no idea what it is the voice wants, but he is driven to a series of misadventures which ultimately clarify his needs. Amid his experiences, he boasts, "I am to suffering as Gary is to smoke. One of the world's biggest operations."

My early adult times at the farm were my African trip. Though not as the world's biggest operation, I did indeed suffer, and as it was with Henderson, some of my misadventures seem comic — and pathetic — in retrospect. But they most certainly were not funny at the time.

In early June of 1972, my first marriage collapsed as abruptly as a steel bridge over some roaring country creek. One morning my wife got up, packed what she could in two suitcases, and called a cab. By that afternoon she was in Boston, gone. I was in a whirl, a delirium of disorientation and panic. For me, the world had lost its center, and what remnants of myself I could find in the confusion were jagged fragments, dangerous uncertainties. This continued though the next year and the next. I was 27 years old when, in late May of 1974, I returned to the Farm for the first of two extended and deliberate rustications, pilgrimages to a place and a landscape and a culture I had only begun to become a part of. I had no more idea of what I wanted than Gene Henderson had: the potential for disaster was large.

By the first week of June, I had taken care of the business involved in settling for a season two hundred fifty miles from where

I lived and worked. I'd cleaned up the trailer, shooing the black-snakes from the kitchen cabinets and the bookcases, sweeping mouse droppings from the sink, shaking out the bags of bedclothes stored in the closet, and disposing of the mummified weasel I found behind the water heater. I'd established a mailing address at the Post Office in Graysville, made plans to paint the trailer and the porch, to rebuild the outhouse, and to work in the pines out the ridge, trimming the lower branches that had been shaded out in the pines' closely-planted growth for the sun. I think I must unconsciously have felt that in ordering the homestead and in tending those trees which grew so simply and so well, I might share somehow in their vigor and climb out of my haunted darkness into a healing light.

Quickly the supplies I'd brought from Cincinnati ran out, and I made the first of a hundred visits to Whitacre Store. My father's work as an engineer for Ohio Bell had occasioned several lengthy stays in Monroe County. He had made friends with Arnett Whitacre, the owner, and several of the folks who hung around there telling tall tales and fish stories, and commenting, often bitterly, on Department of Agriculture policies in Wayne National Forest, which occupied huge portions of the county and which entirely surrounds the Farm. I pulled into the lot in my pale blue Pinto, and the fellows on the porch perked up. Here was a new face, fresh mettle to test.

Arnett recognized me when I told him my name. He introduced me to Chester Piatt, a friend and former worker at the store, currently custodian of Graysville School. There were a couple of other men, too, and far down at the end of the porch, sitting by himself and grinning, a character I came to know better than any in the county.

Arnett wasted no time setting in on me, gently, of course, but testing, always testing. We sat down on the seats fastened to the wall, and he let drop a tidbit he'd run across in his reading. "One in ten thousand babies born," he said, "is born with gills. They clip them off when they're a day old."

"Yessir," one of the other men said. "I seen a jar full of them baby gills once, down in Parkersburg. Years ago. Looked like flowers, they did, but you could tell that they was human."

"How's that?" someone asked.

"Because," the man answered, scooting back in his seat. "They didn't have no roots."

At Whitacre's that morning, I bought—I wrote it down in my notebook for the day—a box of 15 amp fuses, three cans of Sexton Pork and Beans, a small jar of decaffeinated coffee, two loaves of bread, a pound of Longhorn cheese (cut with a huge and mystically sharp butcher's knife from a wheel that lay under a piece of moist plastic wrap on the counter), a pound of ham bologna, a ten pound sack of potatoes, three pounds of onions, a gallon of milk, a dozen large eggs, a pound of margarine, a tin of assorted fish hooks, six various-sized plastic bobbers, a cane pole, a 12-ounce package of bacon, two cans of fruit cocktail, a jar of French's mustard, a can of hominy, three oranges, and four dollars' worth of Quaker State gasoline.

What else I could have bought (but didn't) would have included: spare chain saw links, galvanized stove piping, hemp rope, shotgun shells, motor oil, sardines in mustard sauce, frozen pizza, ice cream bars, ten-penny nails, carriage bolts, horse worming elixir, mousetraps, gloves, work shirts, dog feed, snow tires, Kotex, any number of Pflueger fishing lures, six volt batteries, a key chain, Rice Krispies, Kleenex, a Clark Bar, electric outlet boxes, PVC plumbing supplies, copper tubing, solder, replacement windshield wiper blades, an antique flintlock musket, plastic drop cloths, porch enamel, a matched set of toy pistols, a pre-World War II Mosler "Rock of Ages" safe, a dime bag of M & Ms, and maybe even the gray 1950 Ford in mint condition that Arnett kept in a shed behind the store, and which he showed me once, allowing as how if I sat in it, straight up behind the wheel, I'd think I'd died and driven all the way to heaven.

That was the good stuff, distracting, crazy, witty, detailed with the wonder of the world. I busied myself with it, trying to steer clear of the depths. But a policy of superficial and almost manic attention to detail is, in the long run, a sorry avoidance. Soon enough, the isolation, the silence—especially at night—began to wear on me. I grew fatigued; my defenses crumbled.

I started awake one full-moon night, sweating, itching with chigger bites. Outside the trailer—I knew, I could smell the smoke of their cigarettes—a couple of toughs were casing the joint, deciding whether or not there was anything inside worth whipping me for. They'd have have been strangers, no one from around there, probably a couple of mean dogs up from the river, running the ridges and drinking beer and looking for a little trouble to spice the night. I lay tensed an hour, hardly breathing. But there was no one around: my loneliness itself, like a secret sharer, had arisen and walked outside. It stood in the remnant broom sedge and loony night, thrilled to frighten me so.

I was, as they say, not in good shape. When the loneliness struck me, it brought fear along with it, and my mind veered crazily off course. One twilight, I found myself standing on the edge of the hill. The sky was deep and blue, like an overturned and luminous enamel pot, and as I looked up, I saw ten thousand caddis flies swarming overhead. They were mating, mating in air, rising and circling, flashing like shards of mica. I could hear the hum and click of their wings, their amorous collisions, and a mournfulness flooded over me like the air itself. I longed to let myself go, that staggering and thought-sick animal of my flesh, and to rise with them, give myself over to their sweet thoughtlessness, their instinctive pairings and couplings. To someone coming upon me in that hour of transport, it would have looked as if I'd been struck with the Rapture: wild, unwashed, moaning at the heavens. I was crazy, over the edge, and I do not know what brought me back, unless it was the fading of the light at last, and the vanishing of those flies, like thoughts of heaven lost, among the stars.

My low-grade, constant anguish must have shown. One day at the store, Arnett looked over to me and said, "There's somebody I want you to meet. Set still. I'll be back." Fifteen minutes later, a dark-skinned young woman, maybe twenty years old, pulled into the lot. Arnett came out of the store and met her and then introduced us. She was a Wyandotte Indian, living with her adoptive grandmother not far from the Farm. We talked, Arnett grinned, and, he thought, that would be that.

But I was not fit for such companionship, not in those days. The wreck of my marriage was a jagged mess inside me, and any movement toward the place its pain still occupied within me threatened new wounds. Ronna and I became friends, but only that. Later, she fell in love with Joe down from Alaska on a visit. Eventually, she and her son and he went back to Fairbanks together, living in student digs while he studied physics at the Geophysical Institute. So the world is large, but at that time in my life I could not connect with it on more than the local scale, and my summers at the Farm were, I see now, an attempt to live life smaller, to try to find some rootedness in a place I could know intimately, a landscape I could practice love on with no chance of treachery or refusal. Besides, I foolishly thought, a place was something that, if you needed it to, could leave you alone.

One day I drove up to Woodsfield and bought a map of the county. No fancy item, it was a journeyman chart, blue-printed on a two-foot-by-two foot sheet. But for all its plainness, it was as fascinating to me as the diary of my grandmother would be, or the journal of a mistress. There they were, the dozen or so hard roads— State Route 26, running south from Barnesville in Belmont County to Marietta in Washington County. Route 800, ending at the river and Route 7 in Fly, Ohio, whose 7&8 Inn I'd shot pool in a dozen times. Route 78, snaking east and west from Noble County all the way to the river at Clarington, upstream from the Hannibal Locks and Dam. Those were the main drags of the county, the routes of milk trucks and itinerant oil tankers and grocery vans and insurance salesmen and whatever bigwigs or tourists or passers-through the county might claim.

But it was the less-traveled byways—the county and township roads, some of them no more than a pair of ruts wandering up from some creek or from the Little Muskingum River to peter out in an overgrown pasture now part of the National Forest—it was those I traveled the most. I burned a half tank of gas, sometimes, never going over twenty miles an hour, and never leaving the county. I'd drive over to Mechanicsburg, then on to Antioch, then descend into the river valley at Sardis. I'd head out to Sycamore Valley, stop in the store there, then drop down on 260 to Bethel, where the tiny high school whose team won a state championship when my father was a boy still stood. Then I'd drive down to Marr and the couple of miles to the Washington County line. I'd drive Dearth Ridge and English, Conner and Stonehouse, Straightfork and Little Injun, Wolf Pen and Cleveland Hollow. I'd run out of road above Cranesnest, and stop at Dogskin; I'd drive from Low Gap to Long Run to Krebs Hill.

I'd get lost and I'd see such things: a man three miles out of nowhere, walking down the middle of a dirt road with an eight-foot two-by-four in his hands; bursting from a thicket along Clear Fork, a half dozen kids carrying cut-off plastic milk jugs full of blackberries; once, on 26, just above Rinards Mills, a flock of seven wild turkeys in the road; once, on a Sunday morning outside Woodsfield, five deer in a pasture where an oil well was working; once, near Moss Run, motionless in the middle of a swinging bridge over the Little Muskingum, the most beautiful girl I'd ever seen, wearing white shorts and a huge blue hat.

Gifts, all of them, and cures. I never knew then—nor could I say now for sure—exactly what ailed me in those days. But the breadth and scope, the variety and surprise, the consistent extravagance of the county were all a tonic to me, and I came back to the trailer refreshed and renewed after such days of going and never leaving.

There's a fine Zen story: an old monk and his student are on a journey. They come to a swollen river, and on the other side is a beautiful girl, afraid to cross. Without hesitation, the old monk fords the stream, takes the girl in his arms, and carries her across. She thanks him, looks demurely in the direction of the novice, and goes on. Many miles later, the student blurts in a bitter voice, "But we are not supposed to have contact with women, especially young and beautiful ones!" The master looks at him. "I put the girl down many miles ago," he says calmly. "Why are you still carrying her?"

I'm the novice of that story; haunted by the feel of Greenbrier and its surroundings, smelling the savors of its landscapes, holding its hollows and rises in the arms of memory and desire, I still carry it with me. And its beauty, its pleasant strangeness, draw me still to some cure that is not forbidden, as it is to the novice, but remains, whenever I think of it, a source of grace and healing.

Three

Grace and healing. Somewhere during those summers I'd run across a passage from St. Paul, that wanderer, and I'd written it down in my notebook amid scattered facts about box turtles and tornadoes. *Fides ex audio*: faith is from hearing. Part of what ailed me in those days was a crisis in faith, not in any strictly religious sense, for I had taken a hiatus from the formal Church, but a crisis in faith concerning myself, my fitness and worth as a human being, and even worse, an erosion of my faith in life itself. In moments of terror and despair I had come to believe that life had failed me—or that I had failed it—that it had not provided me, as it surely did the pines along the ridge, or the lilies growing at the head of every gully along Greenbrier, with the appropriate environment, the fertile ground for growth and health—or that I had not lived freely enough, hopefully enough, to find such a place for myself.

Whatever the reasons, my life in the city had grown routine and spiritless: teaching two hundred students a day, jammed into six 42-minutes periods, with interruptions averaging two or three per class, deadlines of a dozen sorts, parents' meetings, committees, preparations and grading, fire drills and phone calls: all of this had come close to disintegrating me. There was no time to think, to consider deliberately what I was doing, nor how my work was part of a whole, not the whole itself, nor to discern what better shape my life needed to take. Rather than acting and living deliberately, I was more or less reacting. I had lost the gifts of pleasure, of healthy leisure, of wholesome wildness; spiritually, I hunched in fear and exhaustion. A bitter seriousness infected my works and days. So it was that an unlikely partnership sprang up down there at the Farm. Earlier I mentioned the fellow I'd gotten to know better than anyone else there; he had sat at the end of Whitacre's porch that first morning, silent, aloof, but even then, for all his carefree distance, his face had been a ruddy wisecrack.

I went back to the store that afternoon. He and Arnett sat on the porch, watching me pull in. As I stepped up, Arnett said, "This here's Jim Winland. He can whistle up buffalo."

I knew that buffaloes were even rarer than the babies with gills I'd heard about that morning. But when Jim grinned around his wad of Red Man, some bitter skepticism lodged sideways within me, unable to come out; I was free to believe.

In a county full of serious farmers, hammer and chisel mechanics, and hard scrabbling laborers who drove sixty miles one way for a job that lasted a week, Jim was an anomaly. In his mid-sixties at the time, unshaven and sunburnt, his white hair brush-cut close to his skull, he had moved down from Martins Ferry, Ohio to fish the county for bass. Stubborn and independent, he flaunted the unofficial dress code of men of his age and station: he wore shorts. They were ancient baggy Bermudas, yellow madras, and they hung below his belly like an afterthought, a kind of sartorial rigging, as out of place as diapers on a bear.

"What you doing this afternoon?" he said, satisfied that he already knew me well enough to ask.

"Nothing, I guess."

"Well, goddammit," he said. "Let's go see us some buffalo."

Jim traveled the county—from Woodsfield, the county seat, where he played euchre every morning at the Wooden Shoe Cafe, to Moose Ridge, where a shack he'd had his eye on to run a card game stood, to Clear Fork and Whitten, Cranesnest and Old

Camp—in a white '62 Ford Galaxy whose trunk he had to jimmy open with a pocket knife. As I stood beside him, ready to hunt buffalo in the hills of Ohio, he talked. "Latch is busted, I'll fix it one of these days. I work a lot on cars. Yessir. And you know how I fix em? I experiment."

He reached into the jumble of the trunk—fishing tackle, two paper cups full of dead worms and dry moss, a tool box, a cracked plastic jug, three oil-stained shirts, a pair of long gray work pants, a wrecking bar, a broken bag of rock salt, two bald tires—and hauled out a pair of boots.

"These here's my wading shoes," he said, pointing down to the Dollar Store canvas specials he wore. "For walking the creek. But I put these boots on for hunting buffalo."

We drove for forty-five minutes, the car bottoming out on roads that staggered up ridges, tumbled down into creek-run hollows, then labored up again, traveling on.

"Hey!" he shouted at one point. "You ever seen anything like this?" He raised his right arm from the steering wheel to show me a long black growth in his armpit. "Goddamn hangin mole. I seen the doctor about it yesterday. Said I'd live. But the thing bothers me, I'll tell you. Like havin a itch-worm in your shirt. Oh, I got lots of things wrong with me," he moaned. "High blood pressure. No wind. Bad knees and deaf in one ear. And I got that strange Hawaiian disease."

"What's that?" I said.

"Lackanookie," he grinned. "Ain't gettin any at all."

We climbed a steep hill out of the woods, breaking onto a grassy ridge. Then a big fence appeared, and Jim pulled off in a wide spot where a metal gate marked with a No Trespassing sign stood gray and padlocked.

"This here's where they are," he said. "Climb out."

He stood at the fence and whistled. Then he whooped three times. Far down the hillside beyond I could see movement. Three or four darknesses the color of wet earth stirred.

"They got elk in here, too," Jim said, turning to me. "And wild hogs. Goddammit they make a racket."

The buffalo came up the hill, six of them and a calf, and within a few minutes they nudged the spaces in the gate like cattle at a manger.

They were hardly wilder than my aunt, but they were buffalo, compact and dense, their flanks matted with dust, their eyes liquid and still. Jim leaned against the gate, sticking his hand through to swat their hides. I stood back, the sunlight heating and brightening the air, a buzzard turning wide circles over the next ridge, the car ticking and cooling behind me. I watched him in his simple delight. For the first time in months, I relaxed.

Fishing soon became the public excuse for our time together. I'd park in Whitacre's lot and walk across the road to Jim's shack and beat on the screen door until he woke from his nap in front of some TV game show. We'd pile my gear in his car, go into the store for a few spinners or a new lure or some bobbers, and then we'd head off down to Clear Fork. Jim had found a good hole there, at the foot of Coy Whitacre's oat field, and we'd fished it several times a week. The banks were steep on the road side, and we'd have to cross a barbwire fence and scoot on our butts down to the edge. Sometimes we'd walk the creek there, Jim in his madras shorts and canvas tennies, I in my cut-off jeans and old running shoes. We'd walk together upstream, working the willows and snags and deep pools to either side. We'd catch smallmouth and rock bass, bluegills and punkinseeds, and sometimes, in the riffles, a string of suckers.

Around the end of June each year, the carp came in there to breed. They'd foul the water for a couple of weeks, but just before or just after, we'd catch a few. Jim caught an eight or ten-pounder one morning, snagging in a half-buried wagon wheel and having to go in to retrieve his pole and the fish by hand. He displayed it in the trunk of his car and drove around the county for a couple of hours, showing it off. Near noon, its gills still gaping and closing, Jim said, "They're tough, carp are. Can't kill em, hardly." And he looked over and said, "Like me."

The private reason for our running the ridges together, and fishing, night or day, every creek and pond for ten miles around, was one we shared, but never named: loneliness. My divorce remained an emptiness in me, and as for Jim, I had gathered over the months that he had no kin save a sister who lived in Shadyside or Wheeling, and, amazingly to me, a son. He rarely spoke of him, and my impression was that they had fallen apart. Nor was he taken too seriously in the county; men who worked hard looked askance at him and at his leisure, and, perhaps, resented him for it. Whatever, we fought off loneliness with fishing and driving, with sitting on the worn metal glider on the porch of his shack, watching twilight climb the hills. And most of all we fought it off with talking and stories, endless stories. Everyone did.

Arnett Whitacre said:

When I was a boy, I was driving down that hill, just past the house. I wasn't going fast, and I seen a copperhead and a blacksnake fightin in the road. Now when a copperhead bites a blacksnake, you know what that blacksnake does? It goes right away and eats three kinds of grass. Nobody knows what three kinds it is; nobody knows that. But then the blacksnake comes back and kills that copperhead. Yes. So this blacksnake went over to the side of the road, and he eat some grass, and less than a minute later, he come back and killed that copperhead. Happened when I was a boy. I stopped and watched.

and

Used to be a undertaker around here, he's dead now, name of Eric Wender. Whenever anybody died in a holler around here, he'd go in the next day in a buggy, totin along his instruments and all. One evening Henry Smith died, and the next morning Eric rode out. Now there'd been some kids, boys and girls, fourteen years old and eighteen or so, been there the night Henry died. So they knew Eric was a-comin.

Henry lived way down a holler, there wasn't no road, just a path. Them kids knowed the path Eric would have to come down, so one of em goes way down in a ravine – you know how them gullies wash out sometimes – and the others climbed a big tree on the other side of the path. Pretty soon Eric comes down the path, carryin them big wooden suitcases. The kids in the trees starts singin, real soft, "Nearer My God To Thee." Then they stop, and the other ones in the ravine pick it up, real soft, you see. Eric drops them suitcases and stares all around him, then he starts runnin up that path. They had a hell of a time stoppin him, too. He says, "I was so scared I was just goin to leave them sons of bitches behind." The instruments, you know.

and

Years ago, they used to have a show up here at the store. They'd put up a big tent behind the house and people'd come for the show. My mother'd kill two or three chickens then, and when the show was over, we'd have a big chicken dinner at twelve o'clock in the night.

Once I was in the tent there, and it was dark, and I got to lovin up Hattie Johnson real good. Started off slow, but then I got to lovin her up pretty good. Doc seen me, and he starts har-harrin, but I didn't pay no attention. In a little while, someone says to me, "Look what's goin on behind you." I turned around and there's Doc lovin up Mary Wingfield, she's dead now. Doc's got his arms around her, and pretty soon he's got a hand on her bosoms. Well I laughed and got back to lovin up Hattie

Johnson. After the show, we's all settin at the dinner table eatin chicken and Doc starts har-harrin about my lovin up Hattie Johnson. Well I was about 14 years old and didn't have no sense, so I says, "Yes, but what about you, a-hanging on to Mary Wingfield?" Doc's wife looks up. She's settin across from him at the table, you see – and she picks up a big water glass – you remember them, Chester, they was real heavy? – and she hollers "You son of a bitch!"and pitches that water glass at him. Would of killed him if it'd of hit him.
    and
    There was this fella used to drive the mail truck. He was married, but he had a girlfiend, and they'd have three hours after he delivered the mail at Graysville. They'd drive out to the end of the ridge and do it. When they came back, that girl'd run right through the store to the outhouse in back. She could have gone around, but she'd always come straight through.
    One day this fella's wife caught on because he was comin home late. That day he'd asked me a about a hound I had, supposed to be a good coon hound but I wouldn't of give five dollars for it. I told him I'd take twenty-five, and he said, "You must be crazy," and that was the last of it. But then he had to explain to his wife why he was gettin home so late, so he come back and give me twenty-five dollars for that hound, and he told his wife he was late because he was buyin that hound off me. That day, his screwin around cost him twenty-five dollars.
    and Jim said:
    I worked at Blaw-Knox during the War. Invented a better way to make the big guns they cast there, and I'd be a millionaire today if it hadn't of been for a boss of mine. Stole my idea, he did. And so I took to drinkin serious. Got hit by a streetcar in Wheeling one night, nearly killed me. After I got on my feet again, I drank hard, and one time fell asleep in a boxcar in Memphis, Tennessee, can't remember what I was doing there, and I woke up in Shreveport, Louisiana. Then I went over to Texas and looked up my sister who was a dietician for the Rice Hotel in Houston. I met a guy who got me to sell opium for him, then I went to Mexico for a while, then I met some millionaire in Lextington, Kentucky. And then I got drunk in some bar outside Philadelphia. This was all in three or four months, years ago. Now I'm here, settin on this porch and talkin. I ain't leavin, I'll tell you. I ain't going nowhere.
    And an old man, stopping by Whitacre store, who'd lived in the same place he was born in in 1891, said:
    I dreamed I was a-huntin, and my dog was fightin a groundhog, and I come on em, and that groundhog come at me. I kicked him hard,

like you would a groundhog, right under his chin. And my wife wakes me up, saying, "What the hell you doin!" Because I kicked her right in the leg. And I say, "I got him! I got him!"

Oh I dream a lot. I could go in there in the store and lay down and start dreamin right away, even in the daytime.

Dreaming. Before we had the well dug in the summer of 1975, I had to haul water every couple of days from a spring about a mile down Greenbrier. Sometimes Jim would go with me, just for the ride. It was common property, that spring, improved by someone years before with a length of iron pipe that gathered its seeping to a steady flow that splashed into a cut stone trough. There was always a white enamel cup on the mossed curb of the trough to drink from. No one ever took it. It was as much a part of the landscape as the hillside above it or the pasture and creek below.

I dreamed of that white cup, dreamed recurringly that an old woman with hair like moss and hands like roots sat there holding it, and when I came up, offered it to me without speaking. And as I drank, she grew beautiful and young, and when I thanked her for the cup, she took it laughing like a girl and said, "It's as much yours as mine. It's for everybody just the same. Just don't take it away. Leave it here. In doing this, you remember me."

Four

Visiting my parents not long ago, I asked to see all the photographs of the Farm that had been made over the years. My father brought out a box the size of a peck basket from a closet, and soon dozens of envelopes lay emptied across the couch and floor. Looking at old photographs is a family ritual everywhere, I suppose, and deserves some comment. If a picture were indeed worth a thousand words, then we might expect a family studying old photos to sit worldlessly, mutely exchanging those images of their past.

No such thing happens. Each picture sets off a flood of reminiscences, anecdotes, geneologies relative to those in them—and often much more. This is the joy of looking at family photos; they are catalysts for recreation—literally—of the best kind, and elaborate histories often arise in these spontaneous moments of sharing.

So it was with the Farm pictures that evening. Those from the early Sixties had been dated in the developing lab—a detail I wish were still in vogue. Below a neatly printed AUG 62, there it was: a talismanic ancestor-picture: my grandfather and grandmother Hague, and Maude Mae Davis Heights, my maternal grandmother. They stand windblown and squinting on the very crest of the knob, the Daughtery house visible in the distance through the REA right-of-way.

I had forgotten that at least once, all my grandparents had journeyed to the Farm. The memory of that gathering renewed again my sense of the importance of the place. Almost every person I'd ever loved in my adult life had been to the Farm. The place grew richer for their presence.

The back stoop, where I first felt the reality of solar energy in one of those pure boyish moments of peace and clarity, had been built, I was reminded that night, by my grandfather. The story is yet another of the renewals and recyclings, madcap and as richly mixed as the gene pool of my family itself, and as wonderfully unpredictable, that the Farm has been the site of for me. That stoop, and the original porch which still survives, were built in part of the plywood my grandfather scrounged from the forms used to pour the concrete walls of the Steubenville Sears and Roebuck store. I hardly remember its construction; I was no older than five or six at the time. Actually, my grandfather didn't salvage the wood directly from the construction site. A bunch of kids from the North End had stolen the sheets over a couple of summer nights, and had built a tree house by the river at the foot of Logan Street. One of them fell and broke an arm; the tree house was abandoned. Pap dragged what he could up over the tracks and stored them against the basement wall until their moment, in the hijinks of time and circumstance, came around again.

But there's even more. The posts supporting that porch were originally (that is, after they were timber harvested who knows where, then milled and sold to the telephone company) the crossarms of the old Graysville Loop-27 line, the original telephone service on Greenbrier. My father was engineer for the underground cable job that replaced the old pole-lines, and he stacked a dozen or so of those weathered crossarms, still bearing their blue glass insulators, under the trailer until their time came around and they rose to service again.

And more. Several of the sheets of three-quarter inch marine plywood that the porch was decked with after some of the Sears material rotted out had originally been shelves in the auto parts store owned by my college roommate's father. Mr. Conly's place stood on Florence Avenue in Cincinnati and is long gone, but the shelves still shed the spring rain after twenty years, and still hold patches of the blue paint I slapped on them two decades ago: remnants more personal and suggestive to me than the faded cobalt blues of the friezes in Egyptian tombs.

Steubenville, Graysville-Greenbrier, Cincinnati: that porch, sun-faded, weathered, warping at its edges, is a memorial to all the places I have lived in and to some of the most important people in my life. How appropriate, for a porch is an elemental thing, only the modern instance of the scoured lip of the rock ledge where our Neanderthal ancestors crouched two hundred thousand years ago, thinking and watching. The porch is the in-between place, the transition between shelter and field, blending the best of both; it is open to the weather and the sounds of the world, but somehow also closed in, having the hint of the dwelling about it. It is the resting-ground, the meeting place, the site of important talking.

This my father knows well. We sat on the porch one summer evening just a year before the birth of my son, his first grandson, and we remembered all the people who had visited and sat there with us. Besides my grandparents, my brother and sister and mother, family visitors included my great-uncle Paul Madigan. Uncle Paul spent several days with me during the hard times, fishing and drinking huge quantities of black coffee. He cussed the chiggers and the rotgut he'd drunk in his earlier years, and in between, he polished the memories of the trip to Ireland he'd made the year before. His wiry, elderly presence there, his enthusiasm and easy-going companionship reminded me again of the effect the place has on visitors. The Farm is a holiday for them. Its isolation and quiet bred meditation and remembrance.

Friends of the family who visited included Don Beam, a Steubenville neighbor and telephone company buddy of my father's, and Dutch Riesling, an expert on snakes, a woodsman and self-taught naturalist who had worked with my father in his line-gang days. There too, had come Ernie Coffee and Irv Cilles and Gale Stem, Bob Gerber and son—all Ohio Bell cronies as well. And Ted Peter had been there, many times. A lifelong family friend, Ted contracted cancer a few years ago. After recovering from chemotherapy, and his cancer in remission, he and my father went to the Farm for a week in the summer of 1986. My father had suffered a mild heart attack the year before, so he too was recovering. They were two survivors then, and they went to the Farm, in part, I believe, for the healing we've all felt there. It was a risk, and it almost backfired.

My father's medication was still giving him trouble. Despite that, he and Ted set out on a hike down Brown's Run, a wild little gully threaded by the remnants of an old logging road. There's a greenbrier thicket on the edge of the hollow down there, and I remember as a kid getting so tangled in it and lost that I was sure I'd never get out. Apparently it was a place like that where my father, over-exerting, passed out. Ted couldn't bring him around. He hiked back through the woods, huffed his way to the top of the knob, and hot footed it down to the road to the Daughterty's place. When they got back, my father had come to, but it had been a close one. Ted and he agreed not to mention it to anyone; the rest of us learned of it, only by accident, more than a year later.

Maybe it was a foolish thing to do, that survivor's hike, but it expresses the meaning of the Farm, and the faith it breeds: there, among the warblers and shagbark hickories, the sun overhead, the big woods stretching as far as you can see — there, my father knows, and I know too, and Ted Peter, and anyone who has been there long enough to feel it — there would be a good place to die.

But it is life that the Farm encourages, and the list of visitors who have come to what was once a near wasteland, previously trodden by perhaps only a dozen human beings throughout its ancient and unglaciated history, has grown amazingly. However the rest of life occurs, however hermit-like the existence of a box turtle or salamander or puff adder, human life seems to aggregate, to clump. For folks from the county visited there, too, once the place became reinhabited by humans. Arnett Whitacre and Jim Winland stopped by several times, sitting in the shade of the wild cherry and sipping 7-Up. And all of the Daughertys, at one time or another, walked up the road: Mary Kay and Jimmy, to bring a bowl of string beans and potatoes fresh from the pot; Chub, to laugh and talk; Gary, bearing a cucumber from their garden and leading the little pony they kept for a couple of years. It grazed on the sweet clover and so made of the once dusty bald an official pasture. Much earlier, when my father first had the place surveyed, Gerald W. "Jug" Sims came too, on official business. He had served in the Army with my grandfather in World War I, and, in 1975, when my now dog-eared county map was printed, had been Monroe County Engineer.

In the mid-Seventies, when I was living there in the summers, I came up with an idea that I regret not having acted on. My father makes it a custom to leave notes in the antique dry sink in the trailer, listing all the birds he's seen during his stay. He doesn't do this directly for me, but there is a kind of attachment between us that is reinforced when I find those lists. I pick them up and scan them, communing through my father's eyes with those other visitors to the place. All of them are natives more properly than visitors, and their names are familiar to me, and as delightful as the human ones. A typical summer's visit list might read like this: goldfinch, wood pewee, summer tanager, black vulture, Cooper's hawk, brown thrasher, indigo bunting, cerulean warbler, chickadee, tufted titmouse, cardinal, Eastern bluebird, pileated woodpecker, yellow-breasted chat, yellow warbler, song sparrow, chipping sparrow, barn swallow, barred owl, red-eyed vireo, crested flycatcher, towhee, red-winged blackbird, cowbird, wild turkey, whipporwill. These lists, these nominations of things, are a kind of eucharist to me. Taking them in, I remember all the variety of the Farm, and the health I've been given there by the light, the weather, the air these actual birds dart and weave and glide through.

So connected with these lists—with the act of seeing, and recording—I had the idea that I would ask every visitor to the Farm to jot down, on a small piece of yellow paper like my father's lists, one "seeing" he or she had been given during the visit. I think I had in mind sightings expressed as poems, haiku-like, celebrating the shapes of sassafras leaves, of the fiddleheads of hillside ferns, the forms of mayapples or pawpaws, the business of bees in persimmon bloom. And I saw these little offerings, these testaments, these homages to the land, all taped neatly under the living room window, or over the valences of the curtains, where they would catch the eye as it wandered over the landscape outside. Or I imagined them tucked like bookmarks into the pages of volumes in the bow shelves, to be discovered by accident, surprising and sudden as the blacksnake that flowed from behind the copy of *Moby Dick* and over my mother's lap.

But my life was too disorderly in those days, too crazy to get even so minor a project together. I am reminded of a sighting I took in dozens of times those summers on the road outside Woodsfield. There, in an overgrown field, huddled like bison under the shade of some trees, stood two steam locomotives, their flanks run with rust, their heavy and startling selves listing toward the creek. Though I have since learned that they are more recent relics, I imagined them at the time to be the last engines of the Bellaire, Zanesville, and Cincinnati Railroad, a line that, amazingly, impossibly, ran through the steep hills and hollows of Belmont and Monroe counties. Locals referred to it as the "Bent, Zigzagged, and Crooked." Rightly so. The 19th century traveler and historian Henry Howe wrote of it in his *Historical Collections of Ohio*:

> It was impractible to build an ordinary railroad through the rough wild country of the Ohio River hills of Belmont and Monroe counties, so [Colonel John H. Sullivan of Bellaire] planned a narrow line with steep grades and sharp curves, and he called it "The Poor Man's Railroad." [It ran] from Woodsfield, county seat of Monroe, to Bellaire...

Riding on that very stretch of road outside the county seat of Monroe where I saw the engines, Howe recounts his departure on the B. Z. & C. on May 28, 1886:

> In a few minutes we were zigzagging, twisting down a little run in a winding chasm among the hills wooded to their summits, the scenery wild, every moment the cars changing their direction and their constant jar and grind, and wabbling now to one side and then to the other.

"Bent, zigzagged and crooked"; "jar and grind and wabbling" — I felt a deep affinity to those lost locomotives. Out there in the field, beyond town, they seemed to me to be resting, weatherbeaten but still solid, and in their hermetic silence they brought to my mind the survivors of some difficult ordeal. My life, when I first came to live those summers at the Farm, had been derailed, knocked off its course. But in time, too, I had found a kind of rest. I too had learned to sit in a field, silent, and be still.

Five

Just a few years ago, I was again driving the township roads far down Foreaker. Coming around a bend, I saw a man standing in the middle of the creek, hoisting an incredible string of fish.

There were so many of them that he leaned backward against their weight, his face red, his hat pushed far back on his head. It was just an instant's glance — the woods closed at once as I drove by — but the scene is one of those images that has become a permanent part of my vision of the place, an archetypal tableau, an icon. The man had mined the creek of its fish; he had as surely exhausted those waters as a strip mine exhausts a pasture. I have reminded myself that I, too, could commit the same error in my relationship to the Farm and its surrounding country. Mining it for detail and meaning, I could be the intellectual equivalent of that fisherman, a greedy harvester who takes and gives nothing back.

So I have drawn back from the place a bit, not only because of new responsibilities, but also out of a feeling that I was asking too much of the place, demanding too much. And there are as a result of my stepping back, still places and details, beauties and extravagances and horrors of Nature that remain undiscovered at the Farm. I hope it stays that way. There should always be some unknown, some mystery never plumbed, in our relationship to a place. To know it too well is to diminish it; familiarity breeds not so much as contempt, but laziness, and lack of respect. There should always be some unexplored next bend in the river; there should always be something more than we can know. Ultimately, the worth of a place is counted not only in what we can get out of it, but equally in what measure of mystery it does not yield, in its reserves of being itself, in its unpriceable natural dignity.

My Alaskan friend comes back from his isolated homestead now and then. He simply appears with no warning after an absence of a year or two or three, after a journey of many thousands of miles. He leaves on my porch a caribou antler, the jawbone of a grizzly, a packet of aspen leaves. He knows I will know what they mean.

It is the same between myself and the Farm. After long and absolute absence, I show up, and it invites me in, the same padlock on the door of the trailer after all these years. I carry the key daily in my pocket, and it is a talisman, an open sesame. Inside, my father's yellow lists sit curling in the dry close heat. On the shelves, the box turtle shells, their scales peeling off, grow whiter. In every window, the bodies of dried wasps and hornets repose like so many mummies, emblems of persistence and change, life and death. I and my family could, at any moment, go there and have a living, a change of worlds. We do not need it, but it is there if we ever do.

What luck to have in reserve another life, another place, another set of memories and associations. It is like having two lives, each of them rich and wonderful in its own way.

The woods thicken and climb; the eyes' pleasure in the long view of two decades ago gives way to the land's close and obscuring increase. My father, in his retirement, watches from the porch the old earth working strongly again. It is why he goes there, the woods closing in, the bald recovered, the life of the place coming back, cradling the knob in birdsong and green.

I am not happy to draw this first installment of the Farm and my family and me to a close. Nor do I feel it is conclusive. The Farm is still an open event, an unfinished adventure. We together, this place and all of us, are one life, the human and the natural occasionally intertwined in a perennial renewal of discovery and connection. I have my own sons' introduction to it to look forward to, their first visit to the place with their grandfather, their first drink from the well, their first sightings of wild turkey and puff adder. It will be an initiation, somehow holy. And I have become, after the years of craziness and despair, the place's minister and interpreter, by my woods-change transformed into something obligated to the rich and strange: may the song of the whipporwill inspire me, may the movement of the land encourage me, may the green, coming back, continue to strengthen and sustain me.

Postscript: June, 1989

Patrick and I have just returned from his first visit to the Farm. His grandfather was with us there; we sat on the porch in the rain, listening to the chipping sparrows and towhees. Each night, Patrick fell asleep to the song of whippoorwills. Even I returned to the old rhythms quickly; the first night there, I woke, as I often did in former years, to hear the barred owl down Foreaker.

Time—past and present—lived vividly around us there for two days. The porch at last needs work; the leg of my chair punched through one of the plywood sheets I'd brought down years ago. The pitch pine that had been no more than eight feet tall when I first went there stands twenty feet high now, spreading wildly, a sassafras seedling struggling under one of its boughs. But there was the same clump of butterfly weed in the yard beyond the porch—not the same, but the descendant of the bush that attracted fritillaries and monarchs from half the township, it seemed, when

I was a boy. We saw no turkeys; it rained steadily during our stay,
and much of the life had holed up, withdrawn, sodden in the hollows. Still, the woods sang their same deep windsong, and the
mists lingered all night.

And we visited the Daughtertys. Back in the bad times, in my
summers of despair and disintegration, I wrote about them and
their place:

Neighbors

To get to where you pitch the horseshoes,
past the blighted garden, up the hill,
you have to pass the house.
It is like a cave in Asia
where the poor crouch hunched on rags
and flies make bracelets
on their wrists.
But from its chink-walled, musty darkness
come all the smells of living richly in this land:
pork grease, mansweat, stove gas.
And on the porch are parts and bodies
of many things,
stacked neat in heaps and bins.
Closest to the door are motors, pulleys, hammershafts
and copper, and furthest from the door,
near the pigshed, stand piles of tires,
refrigerator coils, lumps of good Ohio coal.
I mention all of this because all of this is there.

And as you stand in the dust and gnats before the house,
Mary or Reba or Jimmy
will shout through the door.
I would like you to see what is there to be seen.
I would like you to count everything twice if you have to,
for time and hope are longer than this country's sorrow,
and some flood may wash all of this away,
and so spare my neighbors' simpler lives.

Still, I cannot blind myself
and go home singing.
Lately, night is longer than my neighbors' sleep,

and the buzzards wheel above their fouled and crumbling
well, and the stones beneath my neighbors' porch
are breaking.

It is a young man's poem, somewhat arch, condescending, po-
litical; and it is an unhealthy man's poem. Its closing notes of despair I no longer feel; I have changed. There is still the debris load-
ing the Daugherty's porch, the same sense of life as struggle and
dark persistence, the same uncertain hopes of jobs, however far
away, the same acceptance of life's chances and withholdings. But
seeing Patrick there among the many grandchildren his age who
will spend their lives out Greenbrier as have their ancestors, generation after generation, makes me understand that despair is use-
less, and that the staying power of that family and that land is all.
Time and hope are longer than Ohio's sorrow — or their own.
Though as I write this, Monroe is among the state's poorest counties, it remains for me, and for the Daughterys, I think, a richness,
a treasure. Their family continues together. The newest addition,
Jimmy's son, who is Ralph and Edna's youngest, was born the day
before we arrived. Already Edna had taken him into her arms and
sat rocking him through the morning.

And Patrick, I want to think, has been taken his first time into
the arms of this land. Already, the rhythms of hollow and ridge, of
the cycles of day and night, are folding around him, comforting and
instructing, deepening his dreams. His first impressions are good;
he has begun to accumulate his own "many things" — a couple of
the turtle shells from over the window in the trailer, a crown of honey
locust thorns, a black swallowtail butterfly found in the road, a
hummingbird's nest, the jawbone of a deer. They will join the gar's
skull, the fossils, the scattered notebooks and lists his father keeps
in his study. Boons, all of them.

So the poem is false, wrong. The night is no longer than our
sleep. And though the porch deck may be rotting, the posts beneath it still stand sturdy, tight to the bones of the land. And Patrick
and I and his grandfather, seeing clearly, counting it all twice, can
once more return to our other homes, carrying the Farm in our
memories like music, like singing.

A Porch in the Country

I remember it at its best, in the light of early evening, before full darkness settled. The sky, arching over the gravel lot, the county road and the shadowed pasture beyond, glowed a bluish white those evenings, pearly as the inside of a mussel shell. On the wandering breeze, faintly up from the surrounding hollows, ascended the calls of the wood thrush, clear and liquid as bells. Closer, in the stands of burdock and chickory at the corner of the lot, crickets rasped and ticked. The smells were of the manure richness of the pasture, the acrid dust of the gravel lot, the alien sweet sharpness of gasoline. The two Quaker State pumps stood silently on their concrete islands, gauges and dials dimmed to masks in the dark. Narrow-shouldered and hunched, the pumps looked awkward there, out of place, like strangers who had just stepped down from a train that had brought them into a far country.

It was a fine, open porch, only three posts rising in its twenty-foot length. Its floorboards, eight inches wide, were nicked and wizened as the faces of men accustomed to hard weather, hard times, hard use. But nailed well, crafted truly, they bore silently and sturdily the daily tread of life.

Bolted to the wall just below the original farmhouse windows hung a half-dozen wooden theater seats. Fashioned of bent plywood and veneered with a wild-honey oak, they gleamed where they'd been polished by the denimed and twilled thighs of a quarter-century of edgy talkers. When not in use, they folded up again, mute and comic tongues.

As much parts of that porch as its timbers and view were the dogs. They had become living and essential features, without which, I had the impression, the porch would have collapsed as surely as without its posts and beams. Mostly redbones, blueticks, and beagles, through the years these hounds had acquired startling likenesses to feed sacks. They could assume strange, lifeless shapes as they slumped almost bonelessly over my boots while I sat there. They were hotter than sacks of grain, of course—more flea-ridden, too, and liable to sudden jerkings in their sleep. But awake, they were studies in patience; I watched flies, untouched, sucking the cold moisture of their nostrils, even pick-pocking with cupped and fringed feet along the red mucus of a drowsy mastiff's eyelid.

The porch was a place where anything could happen, but hardly ever did. Hours passed without traffic, trade, or refueling. For whole afternoons, murmurous with the intermittent drone of a distant tractor, the only business conducted in the vicinity consisted of a hundred arrivals and departures announced by clatters and shrieks in the martin box across the road. Now and then a blacksnake, driven by an antique hunger, glided swiftly beneath it, a whip of iridescent oiliness that flowed into the roadside weeds, leaving in its wake a fervid womanly musk that lingered on the air.

A pleasant aloneness rose from the dust and quiet of that porch. It was a solitude made the sweeter by the knowledge that it would not last. For when something did happen, it happened with all the vigor and mix of a sudden parish picnic. Drawn from homesteads in the timbered hollows or from the neat ridge-top communities of eighty or a hundred souls—from Broomstick, Cranesnest, Greenbrier, Old Camp, Graysville, from Dearth and English and Pleasant Ridge—folk convened for something more than the necessities of sugar and salt and society. The country store—this one at least—served, it seemed to me, many of the same functions as a church. On its porch, scattered kin gathered, their sudden meetings all the more festive for their unexpectedness. There, shy smiles lit and spread among the young ones. There, hard times were given their painful, amen-punctuated testimony. Articles of faith were exchanged among believers, sober recitations of miracles, providences, wonders: hoopsnakes, mermaids, a man who could whistle and call not only goats, but groundhogs and even buffalo, some said. Other times, in calm tones, the sternest of judgments were meted, and the common communion of life passed from soul to soul with a devout, plain-spoken reverence.

Things never got too somber, though. Politics would come around in the talk, and speakers' tones would shrill, like banjo strings tuned up. Someone would hit a lick here, another one there, and soon a full breakdown buzzed and twanged among them. Or some young buck would fishtail into the lot, throwing gravel from his radial whitewalls, and, once he'd gone inside, would provide the subject for a series of mordant homilies delivered by ball-capped preachers who remembered Hoover.

One evening, a huge man pulled into the lot aboard a relic pickup. He hove himself from the cab, and without looking over to the porch, marched back, rattled down the primered tailgate, and stabbed around in the bed with a stick as long as a rafter. When he pulled it out at last, a snake no larger than a bracelet hung from its end. "Copperhead," he announced, and approached the porch. Four or five men stood to look. After a time, one of them, a bald octogenarian in overalls, demurred. But before long, all nodded in assent, judged it a symbol of the wilderness's return to the county, and recited copperhead scripture among themselves for an hour into dark.

The theme of wilderness came up often there; it still does. The county had suffered more or less anonymously the general demise of Appalachia. Kentucky and West Virginia got more press, but the boom and bust cycles of coal, oil and gas had taken their tolls there, in southeastern Ohio. People were uncertain about the wilderness. For several summers, a Youth Conservation Corps camp just down the road had been full of city kids come to plant walnut and white pine, and to build hiking trails along the ridges. The government had bought up then demolished dozens of old homesteads for the National Forest, and what once had been bottomland oat fields and corn patches or gentle hillsides sown to timothy or alfalfa now bristled with black walnut polewood and pine saplings. No one felt right about the government's destruction of homesteads, even if the places had stood abandoned for years. A homestead is a homestead, and its disappearance alters the mindscape as well as the landscape of the natives. So the discussions of wilderness were frequent, inconclusive, and generally nostalgic, though with a surprising twist. "This place is getting to look like it did when the pioneers first come," a man complained on the porch one evening. Those gathered there shook their heads in dismal agreement.

I was of two minds as well; I still am. I saw the hardships hard land created: the poorly productive potato fields haggled into thinly-soiled ridge tops; the dilapidated housing here and there; the late night pickup clattering its occupant—in rain or snow, sickness or health—to a distant and temporary job somewhere thirty miles down river. I saw a few marriages killed by want, bad health, lean times, and lack of opportunity, and the three- and four-generation families living among the necessary carcasses of a dozen cars cannibalized to keep the one find-work car running. I saw that the difficulty of small farming, and the buying up of land for the National Forest, and the uncertainty of mining, oil and gas speculation, and spotty timber exploitation were all contributory factors to the judgments of the elders on the porch who bemoaned the wilderness's return.

Yet at the same time, I was not alone in being invigorated by the reappearance of the wild turkeys in the hollows and on the ridges. I was fascinated by the Fur and Roots store down on the river where ginseng and muskrat pelts were being bargained smack in the middle of the Space Age. I reveled in the unspoiled stretches of the Little Muskingum and Clear Fork and Sun Fish Creek. The honest and powerful silence of Greenbrier Ridge calmed me, and the appearance of the Milky Way over that clear and breeze-cooled knob was a lesson and reminder.

But I am also—even more now than in those days—acutely conscious of the fact that I am, and always have been, a kind of outsider to these issues, these landscapes, these folk. Though born in Appalachia (at its very border—had my family lived just 30 miles to the west, we'd have been undoubted Midwesterners), I was not conscious of being of the region. Nor were many of my townsfolk in Steubenville. To have suggested to them that we lived in Appalachia would have brought laughter—or worse, denial. Gradually though, after I left for college, I began to understand in myself certain unsatisfied longings. Specific images—of the porch, its talkers, the countryside around it—became insistent in my memories. Distance had begun to define for me some of the place's meanings, and I thought in new ways about it. Finally, I returned.

And back there, during a couple of summers, I remembered often a man I had met years before. My father had taken me to see him during one of our countless trips into the boondocks during my childhood. This man lived far back a township road, and his place, I had been delighted to learn, required the crossing of three bridges, the last of which was covered.

I can't remember very precisely the appearance of this man. He was short, stout, and the skin of his wrists and face was of the same rich rust as the inside of peeled sassafras bark. He told us with a grin that he was Post Master, Justice of the Peace, and oldest resident of his settlement. Shortly after leaving, it had become evident to us that he was its only resident as well. His was the only dwelling for upwards of half a mile in either direction—my father never took the same way twice on those trips; coming and going were separate adventures, each with its own possibilities. It would not do to waste them.

But I do remember the man's voice. It was a compound of gravel and oil, a rattling slipperiness over which his words flowed like mine tailings in a sluice.

He told us, informally, ramblingly, his personal history of the place. At the turn of the century, the hills surrounding his homestead had been covered with hundreds of oil derricks. Taverns had filled with men every night. Fights had broken out. Marriages had been made. Deaths had happened.

Looking out over the railing of his porch, I had tried to imagine what it had been like then, but I couldn't. I saw cedars rising stubbornly from scoured hillsides and in ditches the rank growth of horsetails and reeds. I couldn't *past* the present; not then, at least.

Still, we sat there an hour, my father listening and smiling, while I studied the debris gathered on the old man's mossed and sagging porch. A refrigerator stood open-doored at its far end; when we left, I saw it was filled with birds' nests. Next to it, piles of wooden milk cases leaned against the wall, makeshift shelves crammed with small skulls, clusters of spoiled teeth and claws, a hornet's nest the size of a football, an ancient pistol, its barrel solid with mud.

But in my innocence and ignorance, I could construct no life from such relics, could piece together no biography that matched these things with this small man's rugged voice, with the rapid and liquid memories that fell from him like the water of a spring. My final impression was that he was slightly loony, driven by long nights and relentless change and mournful isolation into a past more vivid to him than the apparent shambles of his present.

I thought then that such a situation was pitiful. But I have since learned to understand it as an anodyne to wild and thoughtless "progress." And I have learned how tightly held such reminiscences must be. There are those among us who are conservationists — or more precisely, preservationists — and what such neighbors preserve are themselves and the substance of their lives. Thus their stories, not only of human beings, but of places, trees, wild turkeys — even of the clamor and waste of an oil boom — are often the stories, somehow, of old loves, bittersweet, elegiac, moving. In a way, such neighbors, and the places they inhabit both physically and psychologically — even the very porches we sit together on — are the vanishing species, the threatened habitats of our human tribe. Attention must be paid.

That is why, on my return years later to the store porch not far from where the man lived, I felt a loss. Yet another habitat had changed; yet another world of memories had been altered.

It is common practice now to do an "environmental impact study" before disrupting a place in the name of progress or improvement. I do not think one was done in this case. How strangely quick we are to overlook the human environmental impact of changes. We spend hundreds of thousands of dollars to study the effects of channelization—o ugly, clunky word—on the Big Darby madtom. So we should. But we accept almost without question (and sometimes with a positive delight that we have at last caught up with the rest of the country) the erection of a fast food saloon, discount gas emporium, or the aluminum-siding, perma-stoning, and re-windowing of a country store's porch. The effects are subtle yet profound. They are equivalent, say, to waking up next to a stranger in bed beside you after 50 years of marriage, a stranger who claims to know you—who does, somehow, seem familiar— but who, at last, is a stranger.

I remember the late June afternoon I first approached the changed porch. The old theater seats were gone; no longer were there places to sit. The freshet of stories that had flowed so readily before was now dried up, gone. People hurried in, hurried out. Even the gas pumps had been modernized, with digital displays that computed the purchase to the thousandth of a gallon. This unnecessary quantifying, this irruption of the perversely precise into what had once been so rich, so deep, so suggestively emotive, seemed cryingly absurd. I hung around for a few hours, waiting for the sun to go down and for the darkness to wash away something of the hard-edged and painful newness. But just as the sky went green at twilight and the first shreds of fog began to float over the pasture, a security lamp exploded over the lot, exposing everything in its garish and aggressive light.

I gave up then; I felt that something essential had been destroyed—albeit unconsciously, perhaps, and with no deliberate malice—but destroyed nonetheless. I got into my truck and headed down the switchbacks toward the hollow, where the hard state road wound its way to Marietta. Halfway down, I passed a fellow on foot, a beer in his hand. He looked over. His eyes were glazed in the headlights, his face expressionless. Just for a moment—but it was an important and despairing moment—disappointment and unease rushed into my heart. I floored the accelerator, roaring by him. Innocence and goodness were gone, the calm and vivid Eden of the porch lost, even the woods no longer familiar, but strange and distant as the Land of Nod. And that fellow back there, that fellow with his grim and frozen face—something miserable and lost inside me feared, and named him Cain.

The Line

The child lay in a plain box lined with quilt scraps. The skin of its face and hands was pearly, though there was no depth to its luminescence. The gray noon light that entered the open door and explored the farthest corners of the room lit, exactly as it did the child, the broken radio, the piles of clothes, the drawer-less bureau stuffed with pots and boxes, the random bundles of kindling.

The mother sat in the doorway connecting the front room and the kitchen. The box containing the child lay across the seat of a wooden chair in the middle of the room. A straight line could have been drawn between the first branch of the dead oak visible across the road, through the open front door, across the folded hands of the child in the box, directly through the heart of the mother sitting just before the kitchen entrance, and on out the kitchen window behind her into the rampage of the woods and beyond.

As the younger boy came in, he instinctively avoided this line, stepping sideways through the door and then sneaking along the piles of oil cans and motor parts that lay heaped against the eastern wall. He marked the gaze of his mother, whose stare seemed frozen to the line. He knew it was a gaze to be avoided, for it was relentless, dangerous somehow. He moved slowly, trying not to draw attention to himself, and hunched his shoulders until he found a niche in the piles. Then he squatted silently, his back to the wall.

Later, the older boy came in. He too sidestepped the other's staring down the line, and clapped earth angrily from his gloves. The mother suddenly looked at him. "Shush!" she cried. Then her gray eyes settled and fixed again on the line. The older boy stepped past the younger into the kitchen where he sat to one side of the line in a broken chair. Soon his eyes closed, though he sat straight-backed, and his breathing mixed with the rustling of leaves in the woods outside the open window.

The mother tried not to remember. That was trouble: mines, falling well-casings, the old car that caught fire on the road to Forrest, the two dead at birth. But memories paced the edges of her mind like skinny coon dogs with the mange, woods-hounds, lean and whining, with dull copper eyes. She could smell them there, at the edge, and she hated again the smell. To get rid of it she gripped the line tighter.

Down Broomstick, the husband dug the grave. He had sent the older boy home. Why, he didn't know. Things happen. He dug next to the two stones of the others. They were small stones, sad. He did not turn from them. The price to pay, he thought. His spade rang against a rock, then slipped off into clay. He leaned on it, pushing, and the earth wedged out and he piled it next to the hole. He looked up from his work now and then to see the creek through the quaking aspens and poplars, and then down again, to the darkness that squared and deepened before him. The price to pay.

The mother, still holding the line with her mind, thought of her father. He had worn the green pants the day he died. She had hung them over the rail behind the barn a hundred washing days. Her mother had sewn them from some heavy cloth she'd bought at Sistersville, and he had worn them on important days. He had voted in them. He had worn them the day she was born. He had applied for the job with the well-rigging company in them. And then he had worn them to town that day. There had been no blood on them. The bullet had pierced cleanly to the heart and he had fallen forward down the Court House steps, and the blood had run from him in a slow creek onto the sidewalk and out into the street. The crease was still in them when they brought him home. And then other things had happened, and others, and then this. All in a line. She could see only the child's feet over the edge of the box, her small shoes white as lime. Then she could smell the dogs again, the sour meat of them, and she tightened her grip once more.

The older boy, behind her in the kitchen, opened his eyes. A dirty glass sat alone in the sink and he realized his thirst. Why did he send me home? he thought. Always questions. It came to him: always questions.

The husband lay his shovel over the grave. Done. He looked at the two near stones. One the spring of the flood. One the summer of the fire. She had suffered bad. The midwife had been the Indian from over on Cranesnest. A handsome woman with skin like polished walnut. She had shaken her head. "I'm sorry," she had said, twice in three years. After the first one, the summer had been dry, too dry. After the second one, the winter hard. What now? he thought. A man don't know a thing.

The younger boy stretched his legs. He looked over to the other. She stared out along the line, her hands clenched, holding it in her lap. What's a sister? he thought. That's a sister. That *was* a sister. His cousin Mary, Uncle Heeber's daughter, that was Buck and Jimmy's sister. This had been his sister, but not for long, He watched a spider step slowly along a piece of kindling, then drop suddenly, drawing a line of silk straight down to the floor, then climbing the kindling again, another line tight behind it. Outside the wind blew and the leaves clattered and several spun in the door and scratched under the chair the box sat on and stopped.

The father stepped into the room. The younger boy looked to the mother. She did not move. Behind her, the older one stood, staring at the kichen floor, hands at his sides.

"We're going to take her now, Marie," the father said.

"No. Not yet."

"We've got to, it's time."

"Not yet, I say."

It would be dark in an hour. The mother sat still, doing her work. She did not like it but she had to do it. She labored back, now, thinking and remembering, straightening and sorting it all. Maybeth Davit, born June 11, 1979, Marietta, Ohio. Died June 5, 1982, Greenbrier, Ohio. This one, poor one. Then herself: Marie O'Hara Miller Davit. Miller dead in the mine—how long ago was it now?—twenty years? Herself, Marie, born April 29, 1939, Beallsville, Ohio. Now mother: Edna Collins O'Hara, born—when was it?—yes, October something, 1897, maybe Bethesda, Ohio. Died three days after my birth, March 1, 1939, right here in this house. And her mother: Susannah Gilligan Colllins, born right after the War Between the States—was it 1867?—Greenbrier, Ohio, the old house that burned. Died 1897, in childbirth, too, just a young woman. Then. Oh my. Then?

She rested. In her mind she stood from the chair and walked across the room and rummaged for the Bible in the box at the bottom of the stairs. She opened it and looked at the yellow pages in the front, the several handwritings, the inks paler at the beginning than the end. Oh yes:

Maude Preston Gilligan, born December 2, 1847, Drumranmee, Ireland. Died, August 7, 1877, Wheeling, West Virginia.

Drumranmee. That had been a place of hills like this one, and sheep and stone houses and fences of rock in the fields. Aunt Bridget had told me that, painted pictures with her words. Drumranmee.

And then the oldest, farthest back the line, though there are more and more, on back and on back however far, all the way back to our first one in the Garden, she was my mother, mother of all of us, how she must have felt to leave that place. Oh my. But the oldest, the first name (where was *her* mother, where had she been, why hadn't they had that Bible, too?: the first, the most beautiful: Deirdre Yates Preston. Born? Died? Yes, of course, but there's no information, None. No word from there...

So. Done.

"Marie?"

"Yes, what is it?"

"It's time now, Marie. Can't wait no longer, it's getting dark."

The husband spoke strangely, the angles of pain pushing and distorting his voice. She did not move.

And so he stepped right into the line. The mother clutched it, held it, and it pulled at her. He bent to the box, began to lift it. The younger boy stood. The older boy came from behind her, stepped into the room.

The mother shuddered, groaned. And the line, like a clothes rope whipped violently at one end, conveyed the wave of her grief outward. It traveled behind her into the woods, rustling the yellow and red leaves, and it traveled out before her, so that the child's hands — impossible and cruel — seemed to loosen and grip once more as it passed, and the oak across the road trembled as it once had, years ago, when the earth had moved. The wave which was her grief traveled on and on, outward along the line, through the collapsed galleries of Number Two mine, through the mice-scuttled foundation of the grandmother's house that had burned, out through Hanley and Gill and Moss Run, out Wiley's Branch and Sheet's Ripple to the river, out through Saylersburg And Jericho and over the mountains and across the Great Water to Drumranmee, out across the waves and troughs of all the handwriting in the Bible and across her heart, burning as it did.

And then, as they lifted the box and so tightened the line, she leaned back, resisiting, and hauled it all in. She gathered it wildly inside her, a great tangle and twist of darkness, and she fiddled with it with the unsettled hands of her grief, spreading its center thin and building its sides, as if a woman working in straw, moaning and making a nest.

And then, with her mind, she nudged first the young one from it, then the older, then this one, poor one, nudged her gently out. Then more sternly, she pushed her husband out. He stood in the doorway, the box in only his arms now, the boys stricken and chilled in the dusk by the road, itself a line curved through the hills and carrying sorrow coming and going, and she told him, the last of them in the room, she told him, firmly, to shut the door and go and he did.

All The Way To China

He appeared out of a mushroom-shaped cloud of road dust that set the dogs barking. When he leaped from his car and stormed up the porch steps, suitcase in hand, nobody knew him.

"Evening, boys," he said. "Somebody die or you just digesting?"

That got a laugh from no one. The man didn't know what he was up against. Ansen Hilliard hadn't smiled at anything for sixty years, and Lem Barnes was born with something missing from inside him, the lack of which made him immune to comedy.

But this new fella—the Fireball—kept trying. His face was red, his neck was red, his ears were red—he looked to be boiled.

"What do you get if you cross a Coke machine with mashed potatoes?"

Lem Barnes spit into the store lot and stared. Hilliard acted like he hadn't heard. I saw that no one was stirred to answer, so to be polite, I said, "What?"

The Fireball winked at me. Then he roared, "A clogged coin return!" His eyes squinched up tight and he got weakly all over, like he'd fall. He got redder, if that was possible. "Haw!" he cried. "A clogged coin return!"

After he'd settled down and mopped his forehead six or seven times with a hanky, he leaned over and began to unfasten the sides of his suitcase. "Listen up boys," he said, "because what I've got to say is important." He flipped a last latch and the thing fell open. Both sides sparkled with strange gewgaws and gadgets. They flashed so bright you'd have thought they were hitched somewhere to batteries.

"No batteries," the Fireball said. I looked at him and blinked. "Lots of folks think these things ain't no more than toys. No sir. These here items run off solar power, the latest thing. All you got to do is set them in the sun and off they go. And I'll tell you this, too: some of them runs off darkness. Whatever you got."

Lem Barnes hitched forward a little in his seat. His hand wandered toward his pocket.

The Fireball picked up a little machine that looked like a

chromed carburetor with wires flying off it. There was a toothy thing on its bottom, and a spark plug on top. "This here's the newest model," he said, putting it down gently in the gravel. He held his hand over it all the while. "When I move my hand, and that there sunlight descends upon this device, I want you boys to watch close and tell me what you see."

He flicked his hand away. I stared. The thing lit up like a jukebox, then began a slow whirl in the dirt. Then it flipped over and balanced itself on the spark plug.

"Watch close!" the Fireball yelled. Lem and Hilliard leaned closer.

"Now!" the Fireball commanded. And when he did, the thing in the lot commenced a blurry whirr, and shot off sparks. It dug itself right into the ground. Little stones and pieces of dust spun off it in all directions. It kept going around faster and faster until we couldn't see anything but a hole. We could hear it grinding and sawing earth a yard or more down.

Then the Fireball waved his arms. The thing quit. He reached into his sample case and pulled out a piece of white wire that had a circle of metal on the end of it. "Solar magnet," he said, and he lowered the metal end into the hole where the gizmo had gone. He plugged the other end of the wire into his belt. "Contact!" he shouted, chuckling to himself, then started hauling the gizmo out of the hole.

When he'd retrieved it, he feathered the dust off it with a brush he took from his shirt pocket. He turned to us and said, "Well, boys? What'd you see?"

Lem Barnes sat still, hypnotized. Ansen Hilliard rubbed his neck and appeared worried. So I said, "Well, what I seen was this thing you got drilling itself into the ground."

"What else?" the Fireball said.

"I seen you make it stop and go somehow. Didn't see no switch. Then I seen you take that magnet and bring it back up from the ground."

The Fireball grinned, nodding his head. "Real good. Real good. For a youngster, you got a pair of eyes." But then the smile fell off his face. He glared at me and demanded, "You see any angels?"

"What?"

"Did you see any angels?"

"No, I didn't see no angels."

The Fireball stood silent. He inspected me close. He squinted his eyes to slits. Then his face relaxed and he said, real soft, "That's right. You didn't see any angels. You didn't see any angels, or seraphims, or cherubims, or elves, fairies, merlins, or sprites." His voice rose. "You didn't any of you see no supernatural beings at all, no magic, no phantasm, no hocus-pocus. What you seen, boys, was Science, pure and simple. The bare Fact. The Thing itself. You was there."

"Yessir," I said.

Down the porch, Lem Barnes scuffed his feet. "How much you take for one of them things? he said, his hypnotized look thawing to a question. "If a fella was just asking?"

The Fireball snapped the suitcase shut. He put one foot up on it, then leaned, turning the gizmo over in his hand.

"What kind of work you do?"

"Mechanic," Lem said. "Cars, tractors, chainsaws—just about anything that busts, I fix it."

"You go to church regular?"

"What's that got to do with it?"

"That's exactly right," the Fireball said quickly. "Exactly right. You were saying?"

"I was saying what?"

"You was saying whether you went to church regular."

"I wasn't," Lem Barnes said.

"Why not?"

"Hell's fire mister!" Lem Barnes yelled, "Ain't got nothing to do with what we're talking about whether I go to church or not."

You could see Lem Barnes was full of the Fireball's stuff. He hardly ever spoke more than a sentence or two to people in a day. It was like he thought he had only so many things to say in his life, and was stingy, didn't want to use them up too fast, any more than he wanted to use up the dollars he carried in a damp roll in his jeans.

Hilliard said, "Lem ain't been to church since he was christened. They wouldn't have him if he tried."

The Fireball clapped his hands together. "Well then!" he said. "That'll do. Fifty-nine fifty to Deacon Slim here, and good luck to him!"

Next day, there was a crowd in Lem's yard by the time I'd heard about it and hitched a ride there. The sheriff's car was parked on the grass, blue lights flashing. People were spread out in a half-circle, six and eight deep. When I elbowed close enough, I could see that a pond was growing in front of Lem's house. In the middle of it a spray of water like a geyser shot up twenty feet. Lem Barnes was standing in it up to his hips, his yellow raingear slick and streaming, his eyes bloodshot.

I turned to the man next to me. "What's going on?"

"Beats me," he said. "Heard something about an oil well, though. Lem Barnes bragged all last night how he'd got this special rig and bit. Said he was going to open up the oil fields again single-handed, get rich by noon. I come over to see. He's got an hour, way I figure it. My brother and some other boys has got a bet on. Me, I'm laying money on his drowning first."

The water roaring up from the pond made it hard to talk, so I walked back to the road. The sheriff was surrounded by three or four men, Ansen Hilliard among them.

"So what'd this fella look like?" The sheriff had a pad in his hand. He was squinting in the sunlight at the old man.

"Can't say much more than he was a short bird, had a red specky nose, talked a lot," Hilliard said. "A shyster, if you was to ask me."

"What was he driving?"

"A Chevy," Hilliard answered. "One of them compact jobs—a Nova, maybe. Light blue, real bright, jacked up in the back—a hot one. Made a hell of a racket when he come in the lot."

"He say where he was going?"

"No sir. He just took Lem's money and run." Hilliard spied me then and grabbed my arm, shoved me toward the sheriff. "This here boy was there. He could tell you."

The sheriff looked at me and turned another page in his pad. Hilliard fled.

"You got anything to add, son?"

"No sir. It's like Mr. Hilliard said: a sunburnt-looking fella, forty, maybe fifty. Had a sample case full of these things."

The roar of the geyser grew louder. The pocket of trapped gas that drove it belched, who knows how far down. The crowd backed off. Two or three men yelled.

"Lord," the sheriff muttered. He slapped the pad closed and turned back. The pond had deepened; the sheriff's car was up to the hubcaps in water. "I better get that vehicle out of there." He made his way through the crowd, yelling over the sound of the rushing water. "I'll get back to you, boy," he warned. "Don't you go nowhere too far."

By nightfall, most of the neighbors and gawkers had left. The pond had deepened and spread, cutting off the road. Lem's house was half under water. The geyser had died down to a gurgle of oily brine, making ripples that flashed in the moonlight.

Lem stood on a stump next to me, trying to dry out. "Dammit," he said, "I wish I'd of had sense enough not to go for that machine. Thought I'd get me a fortune up quick and move to Florida. Now look what I got."

I followed his eyes back over the pond to the shadows of the house. A tractor seat showed above the water next to the porch. Here and there sticks and boards and a fencepost or two twirled aimlessly in the turbulence.

"And I wish I had that fella's neck right here in my hand, because I'd twist it good. Course he ain't nowhere to be found. Them kinds is like that. Come around, cheat folks quick, then scram. I don't expect there's no warrant in the world could catch him. He probably just got in his car and drove down the road a ways and when he was out of sight, turned himself into a snake and crawled under some rock."

Lem labored down off the stump, hand on my shoulder, and sagged to the ground. He pushed his legs out before him. "Sometimes," he said, looking up at me, "Sometimes folks is plain mean."

Then his eyes closed. The flesh hung gray off the bones of his face. His breath came shallow and quick. I pulled myself away, legged it up the road above the pond and headed home.

I woke up cold in my clothes. It was still dark. The house rattled with the remainders of a telephone ring. My brother came in and said, "Get up, boy. There's more trouble over at Lem's."

We went downstairs and out into the night and got in the truck. A whippoorwill mourned somewhere far off, and a shroud of fog lay over the rich mounds of the garden.

When we came around the bend before Lem's house, a deputy leaped into the road, waving a flashlight. We stopped. He looked in, saw me, and pointed us on.

We pulled up by the pond. Out in the middle, we could see a yellow rubber raft with three men aboard, all pointing their flashlights at something dark floating just beyond them. As we got out, one of the men in the raft leaned over, another holding him by the back of his belt, and grabbed hold of the floating thing. The third man paddled them slowly ashore. The deputy from up the road came running. They all pulled the floating thing up on the ground, and then something like an explosion went off, and then another, and then the sheriff was standing before us with a camera in his hand and saying something to my brother. When my eyes got right again after the explosions I saw Lem Barnes's body being folded into the back seat of the sheriff's car. Then there was the long drive behind it into town and questions and strangers working quietly in the office and the crackling of the CB and then the ride back home, my brother silent and the sun strange and golden and bright, too bright, on the morning road.

That was weeks ago.
It seems a lot longer than that.
Me and my brother and family, we don't talk about it. I had to answer some questions for a week, then the sheriff's office stopped calling. I was tired for a while, but now I'm getting better, I guess.

But at night, sometimes, I wake up and I think that I hear that machine, whirling away deep under the county. I can feel it, faint as anything, humming the bedsprings underneath me, and I can't get back to sleep. And I get this feeling that one of these days something is going to happen, like maybe that thing will dig itself clear through the world, dig itself all the way to China, and it'll bust through somebody's house or something, maybe wreck some fella's garden, wake up somebody important. And they'll find out that it come from Greebrier County, Ohio, and then we'll be in for it. Because nobody I know here speaks Chinese, and misunderstandings will fly all around, and before you know it, there'll be some guided missile or something falling out of the sky, and I'll want that Fireball character to be here so it lands right on top of him. I want to see that. I want to tell them Chinese, "It was him. It was the Fireball that done it. We didn't mean no harm."

But I bet you I won't get the chance. I bet you there ain't nobody anywhere that would listen. I bet you Lem Barnes figured that one out. I bet you there ain't nothing but trouble coming for a long way down the road.

Pool In The Hinterlands

One

The first pool I ever shot was a fast game of nine-ball at T.R.'s, a dusty and fragrant establishment next to the old Greyhound bus station in Steubenville. I think it must have been a Friday night; I was fifteen; I lost miserably. Only moderately obedient in those days, and more than a little cowardly, up until then I had heeded the warnings that were so frequently and from every quarter directed at me that they seemed almost atmospheric, like the mill smoke and dust that ruddied the skies around town. I resisted the attractions of places like T.R.'s and felt righteous.

After all, pool halls were bad business; unsavory types hung around in them, aged mafiosi wearing blood-stained trench coats and hundred-dollar shoes, sitting by the untraceable pay phone in the back room, waiting to call in contracts on slime-bag rivals. And there were plainer, more secular hoodlums, too: dropouts and throwouts from high school, young punks with faces as pocked as asteroids, with skinny dangerous arms, assassins who wore narrow fake alligator skin belts and cruel pointed shoes that could puncture your lungs if they caught you just right in the ribs.

That's how the stories went, anyway. They were calculated to scare the bejeesus out of kids, and for a long time they worked on me. I entered T.R.'s that first night with sweating palms and a certainty that not only would my father find out, but that he'd get me for it.

At least I wasn't alone. Three of my friends swaggered in beside me; I realize even now that we merely quadrupled the fear. But the chemistry of boys is volatile. The catalysts of milltown machismo and the universal and desperate derring-do of young males in packs made backing down impossible.

Terror confused me at first, as if fear had been translated into blindness. I recall my immediate impressions, which were of the place's smells: stale leather of the ancient tables' pockets, dull sours of sweat, alcohol, old cigarette smoke. These smells, ever since, have been magical in their power to evoke my entire youth in Steubenville. Even now, shopping with my wife in some fancy big-city boutique, wandering among expensive leather purses, I am seized with visions of stripes and solids gliding toward webbed pockets lost in shadow. I drift off, and I am sure there comes over my face a vacancy, and almost always I do something clumsy, tripping over my own feet, say, then bumping into a spangle-haltered sales-person who wears lipstick the exact scarlet of the three-ball.

But as Whitman, that New York City pool-shooter says, "All truth waits in all things." All whippings and embarrassments I have suffered over the years have been worth it.

That initial game, really a lesson, underscored my dismal game. My bridge was wimpy, and my stroke, my friends pointed out with snickers and hoots, was more a nervous stutter than a confident glide. My knowledge of rail shots was as minuscule as my knowledge of the intricacies involved in detaching, even with willing cooperation, certain gymnastically gifted young ladies from their brassieres in the back seats of parked Chevys. So I mostly got to stand around that night, at first watching my friends slop and English their ways through nine-ball, and at last, to look around and take in the scene.

I was a veteran of the world of work by then. I'd started clerking at fourteen in the Junedale Meat market, just around the corner from T.R.'s. In a manner of speaking, I was well off. I had a set of parents to whom my gainful employment was not only admirable, but practical as well. My dad's job didn't pay as well as the mill, there were two more kids after me to school, and so on. Working, I could sock away a little money for college, and at the same time pay my way in those pursuits of adolescence which required a little cash. To my family these small things made a difference.

Suddenly, in T.R.'s I realized this. It came to me that I was not only frittering away potential college money (though at ten cents a rack, not too swiftly), but more reprehensibly, I was doing it in a den of iniquity, rubbing elbows with crooks, tough guys, and fel-lows who not only had flunked algebra, but who would roll it if they met it in an alley.

Fortunately, the adolescent attention span, especially when po-tentially tragic miscues are imminent, is blessedly brief. Before the fear completely overwhelmed me, I noticed that the fellow racking for my buddies was the same one who showed up in the butcher shop every afternoon, and to whom we had given the name "Chicken Man."

Steubenville, like any small town, I suppose (though I believe there has been no place exactly like Steubenville, ever) had its collection of what my grandfather called "characters." Along with the Chicken Man—about whom more later—there were a couple of other notables, each singular and astounding in his own ways.

Whenever I tell people of these fellows, they listen at first with a kind of supercilious delight, smiling as they would as some bizarre pet-segment on a late-night TV talk show. Soon enough, though, their eyes roll back in their skulls; they become lethargic, blue about the lips and jowls; some are struck with fits of coughing and dab at their eyes with hankies. I can say no more than this, however: I was there. I saw these men. I spoke to each of them.

Bible Bill cleaned windows. His equipment was installed in the pockets and loops of the overalls that tented his ample and suffering heft. On his left he carried a standard commercial squeegee, while on his right, he displayed several white rags, stuffed like the flags of surrender into his back pocket. He carried a bucket, of course—a good galvanized number, Wheeling Steel all the way. And there was his long handle, borne like a javelin in his left hand, upon whose threaded end the squeegee could be quickly installed. He wore a uniform of sorts which never varied, season be damned: a pair of suspendered overalls, brown boots, white cotton t-shirt. Period.

To us high school students, waiting at Fourth and Market Streets for the West End bus, the man seemed alternately lucid and garbled. One morning he would be the model of decorum, speaking in soft tones to the girls, greeting the boys with a friendly jibe. But the next morning, he might have jekylled, become a maniac. Thunderously, he called us to our accounting. "You reading your Bible, boy?" he demanded, yelling over his shoulder as he cleaned the bank window. "Dammit, you better, you little shit!" Or, "Jesus Christ, girls, what will you say to the Lord?"

He genuinely frightened us; his explosive and unpredictable railings set us on edge. We covered our fear with wisecracks and insults, baiting him, egging him on, then retreating into the Gray Rexall drug store for safety.

Doggy Daddy was another story. He was as thin and hatchety as Bible Bill was florid and bibulous. There was a tautness to Doggy's being that suggested a canine, street-wise hardness, an

uncompromising severity in his razored sideburns and the tight-
ness of the skin across the bones of his face. He always looked as if
he'd just shaved.

He dressed, in that twill-and-corduroy town, like a million-
aire cowboy. I suspect that the elaborately worked boots he wore
were handmade. His suits, too, were of the western cut, meticu-
lously tailored, and all his hats Stetsons, and the gem on the burl
of his string tie surely was of genuine turquoise, twice the size of
my thumbnail.

Doggy's credentials for characterhood arose from the ritual
which earned him his name. Sauntering into the crowded butcher
shop, among twenty or thirty milling ladies jostling before the cases,
he would carefully remove his hat and smooth his hair.

Then he would bark.

And it was no whining lap-dog yap that he sounded. No— a
full-throated mournful bluetick yodel issued from him, followed
by a quick series of exclamatory woofs, as if he had surprised himself. This drove the women into frenzies of disgust. His display
accomplished, he turned on his heel and exited, headed for the next
performance.

This was, as far as I ever knew, the man's sole employment.
All day he roamed Fourth Street and Market, east and west, south
and north, dropping into the McCrory's Five-And-Ten or Isaly's or
Bazley's Market to bark. Where he lived I never knew. For that
matter, I do not know whether he was native to Steubenville, or an
immigrant. But the mystery of the man and his motives was delightful; to consider seriously such a madcap and apparently point-
less self-indulgence was rich stuff for us. Doggy Daddy represented
a temptation to live recklessly and unaccountably, balancing our
milltown work ethic and our families' clambers up the social scale
toward the comfortable middle class, with a little lunacy and feck-
lessness, and I am glad of it.

The Chicken Man was the third in this triumvirate of the
strange. He'd come into the butcher shop every afternoon at closing time. His stained trench coat buttoned to the chin, even in July,
he'd stand in front of the case, clutching the frayed handle of a
shopping bag. Before him, blazing in their yellow fatty chill, lay
three dozen frying chickens, stiff in spills of crushed ice.

"Want to see a chicken!" he'd shriek. "This one, right down
here!"

Some people wash their hands over and over, loony as Lady Macbeth. Others keep looking over their shoulders, even as they lay down to sleep. Still others have a fetish for thigh-high black stockings, or poodles, or Tuesdays. For the Chicken Man, it was chickens. Every day he'd come in just at closing time, when we were busy emptying the cases for closing, and he'd trap us in his bizarre ritual. He'd make us plunge our raw hands into that jagged ice time after time, oblivious to our curses and wisecracks.

"Hold it up!" he'd yell when we'd pulled it out, and we would, elevating the cold corpse in the neon light.

"Now turn it around! Let me see it behind!" His voice by then would have built to a shrillness that crackled and broke up like a radio transmission in a thunderstorm.

"Now weigh it!" And when we did, and when we sang out the poundage and the price, he'd laugh, and spin, his shopping bag flying out beside him, and dash madly across the store and out, never buying.

To see him in T.R.'s then, in the smoke and dim light, the trench coat still buttoned, and him moving from table to table at every "Rack!" intoned from the murmuring darkness—it was an education. In part, the Chicken Man's existence, like Doggy Daddy's, taught us about our marginal selves—about the ultimate fragility of mind and flesh. Where Monsignor Grigsby, the pastor of my Irish Catholic parish, there among the incense and chants of High Mass, represented one state of man, the Chicken Man represented another. Nor was it a mere hierarchy. It was something far more complex. The Chicken Man was a spiritual being no less than the monsignor; the smoke and stained felts of the tables, the hushed voices, the mystical clack of the balls—all of these the Chicken Man attended as a kind of acolyte. "Why are holy places always dark places?" C.S. Lewis asks. That they are is as true of pool halls as it is of ancient shrines cut into living rock and splashed with human blood.

The Chicken Man—the questions darted across my mind like trapped bats—was he priest, wild man, neighbor or pariah—or was he God himself, just as we had been taught in school to believe everyone was? What would the nuns have said had they been there, that night, amid the smoke and sweat of men shooting nine-ball while the Numbers King sat in the shadows by the phone and the Chicken Man, unshaven, shaking, collected dimes from boys frightened to behold his face?

Two

I don't know how much later — maybe fifteen or twenty years — I found myself at the bar of the 7&8 Inn, a roadside establishment at the junction of Ohio Route 7, the state's major eastern river road, and State Road 800, one of the most scenic in the region. Where the roads meet, the bar leans like a weary shrine, and for a few hundred feet upriver and down from it sprawls the town of Fly. According to the gentleman named Walter with whom I had just spent an hour talking, and whose grandfather used to bring the mail in a johnboat from the railroad across the river in Sistersville, West Virginia, the town got its name around the turn of the century as the result of applying to Washington for its own Post Office.

"A bunch of the old-timers around here got together to vote on a name," Walter said, adjusting himself on his chair. "I believe it was down at Solomon's store on the river, but I could be wrong. Anyway this fella called Jimmy — I disremember his last name — this Jimmy, anyway, was there, and he couldn't hear too well. While the rest of them was arguing, he got to swatting at a fly. It was the devil of a fly, and old Jimmy, he wasn't getting the best of it. Finally he just shouts, "Ah dammit, fly!" Just like that, you see.

"Well, all of them other fellas left off their discussion and looked over. Being as how this Jimmy was the senior member among them, and being as how they wasn't getting nothing agreed on among themselves, they all nodded — that'd do. Besides, the government told them to get the shortest name they could. So Fly was it."

"I don't know about that," said a woman in the local school for special students, just down the road from Walter's place. "I can't verify or deny that story. But I can say this. I called Chicago today for some supplies from a company there, and when I told them where to ship the stuff, they said, 'Now that's a heck of a name.'

"But you listen here, young man," she said, smiling and leaning toward me across her desk. "My son's a school teacher over to Cairo, Illinois, you know where that is? Well he told me once that Chicago means "the stinking place." It's an Indian word. I reckon when you get down to it, Fly isn't half so bad as a person might think. Relatively speaking, you understand."

The 7&8 Inn had a used, familiar feel to it. It was to saloons as a camper cap is to a pickup: a bit roughed up around the edges, dented here and there, maybe missing a window crank or two, but solid, still able to keep the rain out. There were accumulations in the place's corners not to be inspected too closely, and torn seats on the stools. But it remained whole, inhabited with real lives lived in the real world. Over the bar a neon light brightly hummed CARLING into the summer air.

Outside, in the spindly ailanthus trees that grew against its walls, a few cicadas ground the air into fragments of noise as sharp as broken glass. Through the open door, I could see across the road down to the riverbank where the Fly-Sistersville ferry had its landing. A man sat on the downriver side, mashing a fist full of Wheaties into catfish bait. Now and then he paused to sip Iron City from a can.

The bartender, tipping his head riverwards, said to no one in particular, "That there Smitty'd rather fish than chase women." A man down the bar, wearing a faded red cap decorated with dust-colored polka dots, grinned and took a long pull of his beer. The cicadas climbed a key; their racket filled the place like the whine of a buzzsaw. A woman sitting at a table next to the door got up and slammed it shut, then sat back down, wiring her gray hair through her fingers. Above us, the blades of an old fan revolved slowly, whispering *wash, wash* over and over in the heat.

Dangerous day: heat, river, beer, idleness, and now there, back in the corner as I sneaked a look over my shoulder, a pool table, its rails gleaming faintly with grease.

I stood from the stool and asked the bartender for some change. The fellows at the bar turned to look at me for a moment. They'd watch, I knew, for a few shots, and then one or another of them would come back and lay a quarter wordlessly on the rail, and the ceremony would have then begun.

Three

Pool is present-oriented, immediate and concentrated; past disasters are forgotten with the first click of ball on ball. As if in a dream, vectors, angles, velocities — mysteries, all of them, in normal life — reveal themselves radiantly with each stroke. I have heard of pool shooters who remember past shots, but I consider them vulgar mechanics of the game, mere empiricists. Pool *must* be revelatory, visionary, unexpected, for otherwise this game, invented (according to one legend) in the 14th Century to bring lawn bowling indoors during the English winter, or according to another legend, brought to Europe in the 11th Century by a gang of crusading Knights Templar, would be as ordinary and predictable as scones and tea.

I am not alone in thinking this. A friend of mine, Joe Enzweiler, champion visionary pool-shooter, agrees with me in every detail. Not incidentally, he is a physicist by training, a poet by avocation. Bound for the Geophysical Institute in Fairbanks at the end of this summer, he tells stories of shooting pool for eleven hours straight, partnering with Kenny Gray Owl, whose strange affectations with the pool cue, and whose odd movements around the table suggested a kind of mad Tai Chi right there in the D & D Bar, local to the Lower Brule and Crow Creek reservations, then afterwards coming face to face with the Great Manito on the highway outside Chamberlain, South Dakota. Poetry and mysticism. The true geniuses of the game have poetry in their blood.

Pool and poesy — what more congenial arts? The harmony of dimensions found in the billiards table (regulation tables are exactly twice as long as they are wide) is as orderly and reliable as the number of lines in a sonnet, and the intricacy of three-rail shots echoes the tense, repetitive beauty of the sestina. Each art requires a sure sense of form and technique, and each equally requires a certain intangible, call it what you will — grace, infusion of spirit, inspiration.

That morning at the 7&8 Inn, however, was not one of such mysticism. It was hot, and there was a pool table, and that was that. The rack there at the 7&8 was sturdy, worn, waxed finely with palm grease and whiskey, and the balls nested smooth and secure inside it. And the cues — the cues! They leaned in a corner, every one crooked or wracked, half of them tipless, the other half split to the handle: drunkman canes, lightning cues. I hesitated a moment with a feeling akin to the awed calm of a pilgrim gazing upon relics. I chose one carefully, chalked it lightly with a cube that rested on the rail at the head string, and leaned over to break. I might even have offered a silent prayer of thanksgiving to the legendary Catkire Moore, a chieftan of 2nd Century Ireland who, it is said, bequeathed billiard balls and cues to his loved ones.

The grace did not stop with the excellence of cues and balls, however. After a few shots, for example, I saw the the rails on this table seemed to be constructed of damp balsa wood. A stiff rail shot traveled a foot, perhaps two, then stalled, as if the ball had run through glue. And the teats — the corners of the the side pockets — were mashed formless, like the edges of an abused cardboard box. The cue ball was an inch smaller than the object balls, this state of affairs adding to each shot a peculiarly upsetting, though vision-engendering, complexity. And finally, there was the light: It hung glaringly from a frayed, ozonic cord, as sensitive to movement as a seismograph, arcing back and forth above the table with my every step. Great shadows moved across the table, burying pockets, balls, even the end of the cue in darkness.

I was in my element. I could not repeat a normal shot — every attempt was a new thing, utterly itself, without precedent or principle. Missed shots scattered across the table like the seeds of galaxies slung from the Big Bang, like a multitude of blessings, an infinity of happy choices.

Happiness, it seems to me, is achieving frequently a period of timelessness, a kind of concentration that excludes almost all of Creation, allowing you to focus intensely on the bit of wonder at hand. Readying to shoot in pool, one arm extended as a prophet's is when abjuring the crowd, the other at the waist, just where the six-shooter hangs, all the while your other hand clenched in a tight smooth bridge, thumb and forefinger touching — when this occurs, and the light descends from the cloudy dimness overhead, and on the table before you, like little models of atoms or molecules, the very building stuff of matter, a two-dimensional simplification of fission and fusion, a kind of cloud-chamber in which you are God and Fate and Chaos and destiny all in one, principal and agent, doer and maker — then life comes as clearly into focus as it ever can, and attention to its sharpest and most vivid point. And to all the potential for order and surprise in this little system, you, with a single flick of the forearm, insert energy, and then all Newton breaks loose.

And what is amazing about this world is that you can be having such thoughts, privately, while leaning over a pool table in a dusty town too small for a library. Hannah Arendt in her study of the Nazi Adolph Eichmann discovers "the banality of evil" — how such an historically large evil as the Holocaust could have arisen in part through the person of so — well, so *common* a man. But the world is tricky in this way, as it is in others. Not only evil and violence, but insights, revelations, glimpses of something of even the glorious and happy truth occur in the commonplace. After all, where, in the world's terms, is it *not* commonplace? To Nature, the Grand Canyon is a yawn, the Himalayas no surprise at all, the Marianas Trench expected. A possible million species of beetles, let alone all the other insects? It's nothing, Nature says, waving it off with a zephyr or gale: Look what I've done with all the extinct species. You think sea slugs are strange, or nudibranchs, or the tubeworms in undersea volcanic vents? Check out the Burgess Shale animals, check out Opabinia and Wiwaxia; consider, as seriously as you are able, what I might have been up to when I created Hallucigenia.

We are close to the truth of the world in any activity we do for fun, however trumped-up our reasons, however absurd-seeming our expectations of such activities. We are capable of kidding ourselves into quite serious things. The sense of play can metamorphose, quicker than a skinny minute, into the sublime. There's nothing more bombastic and bullying than a summer thunderstorm; tell that to J. M. W. Turner, and he's likely to crank out a masterpiece of awesomely beautiful commotion, glimpsing in that same weather the face of God.

Physics, divinity, grace, the sublime, and bending and bowing in the darkness and sweat over a dusty pool table at the edge of Appalachia. You can get just about anywhere by starting just about anywhere. Even a game of eight ball might be the ticket.

Four

I have never lived in a suburb, either a pyschic one, or an actual one. My world has never been homogeneous, but always varied, eclectic, ecumenical. It's not that Steubenville was original or unusual in its diversity; the town was still in many ways segregated when I was a boy, and various species of intolerance and ethnic exclusion maintained a foothold there. But in my home town you could, in the space of a ten-minute saunter, catch a baseball game on the TV at the Polish Athletic Club, stop in at "The Luth" or Lithuanian Club, and then drop down to the Roma Bar for a beer. On the street, you could see fat burghers from the westernmost farms of the county, and right alongside them, Appalachian coal miners and millworkers from West Virginia. Browsing through a recent edition of the Steubenville-Weirton phone directory, I find the following names, a carol of America which would have inspired Whitman, and whose full beauty and effect cannot be experienced unless you say them slowly, out loud: Madden, McPherson, Makricosta, Moleski, Manfresca, Mantica, Manypenny, Marciniak, Mascolino, Maslowski, MiCucci, McConnaughy, McCormack, McCoy, McCutcheon, McDaniel, McDevitt, McDiffit, McDonald, McDonough, McDougal, Mulrooney, Miezkowski, Milosh, Mikedis, Miriankos, Misselwitz, Morgan, Moses, Moscato, Mrvos and Myslinsky. —Speakers of Eight Ball and Nine Ball all of them, of the universal vocabulary of scratch and rack and slop: fathers and mothers, sons and daughters, cousins and nephews of pool shooters. (And yes, there are Moores—descendants of Catkire Moore, perhaps, one of the inventors of pool, and Carrs, too, maybe descendants of the very Originators, those demigods of pool legend.)

In places like Steubenville and Fly and Follansbee, West Virginia, I think I know something of the attraction of pool. All these towns are in rugged hill country, located in the midst of the Pennsylvanian geology, bearer of the great coal seams of Appalachia. The deep mines, and more recently the strip mines, have for generations laid waste a whole landscape's beauty and wounded a whole people. All the creeks I knew as a boy were spoiled with run-off, and the high sulfur coal continues to acidify the rain that eats forests. Much is ruined. So we instinctively remember, and long for, the unspoiled geometry of the old original swamp, that great green breeding shallowness whose fossilized remains run deeply — or not so deeply — under our feet. A pool table, in its level greenness, may well be the flattest place around, the only way of attaining to something like that ancient and humid sea-level in the whole region. We can't help ourselves; surrounded by confining ridges and high walls and slag heaps, and the din of mill and railroad and coal truck, on the felt expanse of the table we get down, we get back, we shoot pool.

Of course, my friend and pool mentor (or is guru the better word here, since there is a spiritual connotation to guru lacking in the more Western, technical mentor?) Joe Enzweiler hasn't got much to do with Steubenville. He is as innocent of the Ville as he is of The Hamptons or Hollywood or Shaker Heights. We first met in 1966 or '67 at Xavier University in Cincinnati. He was a physics major and a poet; we wound up in a literary fraternity together named after the Mermaid Tavern of Elizabethan London. Together we listened to Keats sing his celebration of the place:

Souls of poets dead and gone,
What Elysium have ye known,
Happy field or mossy cavern
Choicer than the Mermaid Tavern?

Over the years, I got to know Joe in other circumstances than writing, the main one being in the Games Room, where Joe worked part-time while hustling a little pool on the side. He's deliberately vague about this, but I think he must have paid for at least some of his college expenses by shooting pool against prosaic business majors from Indianapolis or Fort Wayne, and I think he advanced to the national level in some inter-collegiate pool tournament or another. I don't want to press him too hard for details, though; it would be sacrilegious.

It certainly was sacrilegiously frustrating to shoot against him; an evening of eight ball would end with Joe having won 15-1. My cursing, sad to say, sank to notable depths in those days; Joe laughed at my blasphemous combinations and my obscene deconstructions of words in order to insert Anglo-Saxon expletives into their interstices. But he had faith; to him, I was a pilgrim, and pool, he already knew, was salvific. If I hung around it long enough, all venality and upset and impatience would be washed away. I would be a changed man.

Nor is it over yet. Salvation is ongoing, as is my relationship with pool. And with Joe.

I remember his mother, a stocky woman with a degree in violin who, later in life, went back to school to get a teacher's certificate, and who helped out in the grade school of the local parish. Sadly, when I came really to know her, she was dying of cancer. During one of my Novemberish bachelor funks, I was cheerfully instructed by this woman to "imagine you're a sack of feed leaning up against the side of a barn. Somebody just dropped you there, nobody's holding you up. Now just slump and settle there, feel every grain of you relax and slide to the ground. That's right, every grain."

What kind of woman was she? By her fruits shall we know her?

Here are her children: Joe, the oldest, *aka* "Cosmos": M.S., physics, from The Geophysical Institute, University of Alaska at Fairbanks, B.S. physics, Xavier University, Cincinnati; poet, homesteader, draftsman, cartographer, builder, mason, autodidact, photographer, ice dancer, musher, billiardist and trencherman extraordinaire.

Phil, middle son, *aka* "Tunisia": M.A., German, Xavier University; concert violinist, teacher of college composition, orchardist, autodidact also, homesteader, curmudgeon, Russophile, gardener, ham radio operator, clock collector and restorer of old buildings.

Steve, youngest: B. A., Communications Arts, Xavier University; harpist, Groucho Marx imitator, once made a cardboard and bedsheet and duct tape facsimile of a NASA spacesuit "exactly like Neil Armstrong's" which he would don and then go out in the yard and move as if in 1/6 gravity, spelunker, Elvis Presley imitator. Once, as a teenager, Steve painted a number of copies, or variations of, the Mona Lisa and mounted them on the walls of the Enzweiler basement, where he practiced saying Catholic Mass. Not to be outdone by his brothers in unpredictability and variety, he is now a United Sates Air Force captain, stationed in England.

Telling anecdotes:

Joe

At one point in our billiardly travels in the early Seventies, Joe and I wound up at the New Dainty Lunch, an eating establishment in Marietta, Ohio. It was a hole-in-the-wall place, narrow, deep and dim as a groundhog's hole, but with a pool table in the back, and Joe and I ventured to shoot a game there. In his admitted compulsion to take careful notes on everything, to put into language as much of experience as is possible, Joe always insists that even a single game of pool be given its name, as if every idle match is a tournament of singular importance. This one was dubbed "The New Dainty Lunch Invitational," (to distinguish it from a later, though locally-related match called the "Fly Open"). As usual, Joe won, 1-0.

But the match was notable for the difficulties the site posed: the rails, the felt—indeed, every surface of the table—were slick with a fine deposition of grease, so that even leaning into one's bridge was a maneuver fraught with uncertainty and danger. I recall looking back at the cook now and then, a cliche' of a man, jowly, wearing a stained butcher's apron, and with a short little smolder of cigar in the corner of his mouth. He stood watching us with his arms crossed over his chest, and now and then released small spurts of yellowish smoke, acrid as the gases from a fumarole, as if he were some sort of human Yosemite.

On a recent trip back to Marietta, Joe and I drove around

town, looking for the place. Failing, we ate lunch (a huge plate of beans and ham, with coleslaw and cornbread, for two and a half bucks) at another Marietta establishment, and Joe inquired about the New Dainty Lunch. After consultation with her manager, the waitress allowed as how she'd heard of the place, but that it had closed several years before, and she couldn't exactly remember where it had been.

Beautiful: the most fitting end to a famous place and a famous single game of eight-ball. Sometimes the lack of a memorial makes the event and the place all the more suggestive, as the Holy Grail or Noah's Ark continue to elude searchers and any final proof, or the site of Camelot.

Phil

I first met Phil around the time I was in graduate school. He was always in his room when I visited the Enzweilers, either playing the violin or suddenly appearing, tall, thin, his straight red hair down over one eye, with a cigar box in his hand, soliciting for the "Tunisia Fund." Phil had an intense interest (I avoid the phrase "obsession with" only reluctantly) in Tunisia, and he rather pointedly panhandled every visitor, thinking to build up a fund with which to travel there. He spoke of the place glowingly, painting verbal pictures of its vast hot wastes as if of some Islamic heaven, and was apt to display his QSL cards from Tunisian ham operators he'd contacted. Phil was the embodiment, for me, of Sherlock Holmes: a tall nervous brilliant person of somewhat eccentric interests whose life alternated between fits of violin-playing and exotic research.

Now Phil lives with his wife Nancy and their two children in a stone house built by some of their ancestors back when Germans were settling the boondocks of Campbell County, Kentucky. The house is built on a hillside so that its cellar, to the creek side, is deep enough to hold a double wide door and high enough for a team pulling a wagon to enter. There are still the remains of the old winery's stone trough and stone benches, and Phil has replanted the hillside in catawba grapes.

All of which is normal enough, given a certain class of modern persons dedicated to reviving the old ways with dignity. But now the oddness — there is always an element of the odd in this family, one of its notable charms. Phil has allowed himself to be known, informally, of course, as the leader of this two-and-a-half acre homestead, has posted a sign on the power pole by the road that reads "Now Leaving The American Sector," and has dubbed the place "The Autonomous Region." Furthermore, in a coalition formed between an ornery nostalgia for pre-glasnost Soviet strongmen and a stiff-lipped German efficiency, Phil has encouraged Joe in the construction of a 785-foot-long field stone wall almost completely surrounding the Region save for the boundary with the road and the creek. Both Phil and Joe can tell you how many stones there are in the wall (approximately 15,000), what their weight is (approximately 190 tons, or almost 38,000 pounds), how many truckloads they've hauled (211). The rock for the wall has all come from within a mile or two of the homestead, manhandled up out of creekbeds by Joe and their neighbor Bob Franzen (who, coincidentally, is married to Alberta Enzweiler). Joe estimates, since each rock was handled four or five times—out of the creek and into the truck, out of the truck, up to the wall, into the wall—that the job required 2 million hand-pounds of labor. I am tempted to claim that only pool shooters have this kind of stamina and perseverance, but I would be wrong: marathoners may match them, or decathletes, or certain African hunters who, it is said, can jog for twenty hours at a stretch without getting winded.

However the numbers work out, it is clear that manually and together Joe and Bob have altered the geology of Campbell County, and probably changed the water table by an inch or so in the bargain. I met Bob one hot spring afternoon as he was spading Phil's garden, a neighborly gift of labor. The hemispheres of neatly turned soil glinted brown in the sun like so many horseshoe crabs, and Bob leaned on his shovel like Poseidon, trident in hand, wiping the salt water from his brow. At the same time, Joe knelt on the far hillside among a spill of rocks, building wall. Phil presided over this tableau of the pastoral like some chief swain, some head husbandman like the pre-Trojan War Odysseus in the meadows of rocky Ithaka, looking out over the sea. The sunlight poured down aslant, as it does in Breughel's "The Fall of Icarus," and there was the same antique and dusty intensity, smelling slightly of fresh-turned earth and goat manure, that the painting evokes. That there are places and moments in the late 20th Century that recreate, if only for a moment, such powerful and golden pasts, is one of the miracles of the here and now, almost as moving as making a four-rail shot to clinch the last game of eight ball.

Five

A human being needs some kind of anchor, an activity of skill that is universally current, a kind of Esperanto of technique that is portable and legal tender—socially speaking—anywhere. For urban types, it might be basketball: drop a fellow from Compton or Cleveland or Harlem into a neighborhood in Sao Paolo or Munich or Yekaterinburg, give the gathered crowd a basketball and a net, and you've got instant international relations. For country folk, it might be ways of tying a hook onto a fishing line, or the best method of curing ham or smoking sausages, or something with knives like mumbley-peg.

For me, it's pool. All the places I've been, all the tables I've seen, all the long nights fading into morning...Joe Enzweiler, reminiscing again about the D & D Bar outside Chamberlain, South Dakota, remembers one detail above all others: the 18 bottles of beer lined up on the piano next to the table. Friendly games in bars are often played for a beer, and Joe had put together a nice string of wins. The problem was that he couldn't—and wouldn't—drink all that beer. I imagine that as the night wore on, and as his opponents saw the line of brews growing longer, a nervousness began to spread among them, and it wasn't over getting beaten. It was over Joe's bad behavior regarding those 18 bottles. These side issues are a crucial part of the unwritten rules of the game, and to ignore them is a serious breach of decorum. When you win a game in a bar, you're supposed to drink the beer.

And if you don't, you can get into serious trouble. Fellows come up to you and say things like, "What's the matter, Fella? Don't like my buddy's brand?" Or they'll hint that your manhood may not be all that it ought to be—that your cue's a little crooked. In roadside joints especially, drinking all night is a part of the skill of pool, and anyone who can't do both equally well is a rube.

So it was that one night, many years ago, at that same crossroads tavern I've described earlier—the one straddling the county lines (and thus in a rather ambiguous position law enforcement-wise, since the jurisdiction divides at approximately the head string of the table; if you were breaking you were under the rule of one county, but if you were shooting at the head of the table, you were under another)—it was there, at that crossroads place, that I got into some trouble.

I was with Jim Quinlivan. We had been at the place since twilight, and it was now going on midnight. We had been shooting partners all evening, and had held the table, in the flush of beer, slop, and genius, for six or eight games in a row.

That in itself is a breach of poolroom decorum, made even the more dreadful when you are total strangers to the locals. It's one thing for a fellow known around town to hold the table for an hour or two, but when a couple of outsiders roll in and hog the action for that long, thumbs, as the saying goes, could get broken.

Jim and I were resting between games when a couple of fellows came up. One of them, the shorter, said, "We'll shoot you for five dollars." He didn't so much offer as he *announced* it to us.

He was a short broad stump of a guy with cruel stubby arms made for strangling pigs and a belly that sagged over the tops of his jeans like a slow landslide. He moved in sudden awkward lurches, like a piece of heavy furniture being pushed from behind. His eyes had all the life of a piece of slag, and he smelled of Barbasol and gasoline.

His buddy was a lean shitepoke with tiny rust-colored eyes like spray-painted bb's, and a sharp carroty nose. His face had slipped a little to the right, like the frame of a car that's been broadsided. You had to stand a little to his left to see him straight on.

We knew we had no choice: either we would shoot pool with those guys, or we would have to leave. Jim and I huddled for a moment, then agreed. The two guys disappeared into the darkness, reappearing a minute later with cues. A crowd began to form around the table. The temperature went up ten or fifteen degrees.

Jim and I shot well, but so did Shorty and Bent. At last it came down to the eight ball, and it was my turn. As I leaned over the table, the crowd pressing in closer all around, suddenly the beer hit me, all of it, a huge foamy breaker across my neck and back. I could not see the eight ball; I knew it was on the table before me somewhere; I reasoned that even if I could not see it, I should be able to see its shadow; I looked and looked, but I could not find it. I slid over to Jim and said, "Where's the eight ball?" He grabbed me by the shoulders and said, "What?" Then he looked at me closely, and he knew. The starch went out of him.

"It's in the upper left corner, about four inches off the rail and three inches from the pocket. An easy cut, but watch for the scratch."

I leaned over the table, but it was like leaning over a hole in space, like hanging out of the window of the space shuttle. Everything was moving, fast, and all was blue and rainbow at the edges of my sight, while straight ahead, I was utterly blind. I could not see my own hand, though I knew it must be out in front of me somewhere, there at the end of my arm. And I knew that upon it must be resting my cue stick, and that the pool table was under them all. Yes, I knew all these things in my reason. But as for the reality—all was as mist or fog. I tried to picture in my mind the leave Jim had described to me, and then—I don't know, I just sort of willed that a cue stick would move, and that the cue ball would travel toward a spot on the table, and that all would be well. I heard a clack and then a burst of laughter like a bubble of gas released far underwater, expanding and shimmering as it rises to the surface and then pops open in the air. The next thing I knew, something green and alive was in my face, shouting something about five dollars.

Over the years, Joe Enzweiler has taught me about one of pool's most subtle dimensions, expertise at which separates the genuine practitioners of the art from mere nebbishes. The psyche (pronounced *sike*) can be the most challenging mental aspect of the game. Joe introduced me, early in my apprenticeship, to such common ploys as the Chalk Psyche, the Rack Psyche, and the Medical Psyche. The Chalk Psyche works best in a roadside joint where there's a noisy and confusing crowd, and involves taking up the chalk and then, while your opponent is at work, setting it back down in some obscure place on the table, or even better, on a smoke-obscured counter full of ash trays and empty beer bottles somewhere near. Your opponent, his turn come up, thus has to break his rhythm, and instead of chalking quickly, all the while concentrating on the table and his shot, has to bumble around, looking for the stuff. If the psyche is exceptionally well-executed, he sheepishly has to inquire of you or some onlooker about its whereabouts. Psychologically, this takes him out of his game, and tips the power scales in favor of the opponent.

The Rack Psyche is executed only among friends. To do it with a stranger would be to invite mayhem. It always occurs as the opponent is getting ready to shoot the eight ball (or the nine, if that is the game, and if only the winning ball remains on the table). As the opponent lines up his potentially winning shot, the psycher takes up the rack and slams it loudly on the table, as if to say "Oh hell, I concede that shot, there's no way you can miss it, it's clear that I have been beaten." Often the appropriate body language accompanies this, and the feigned despair breeds the desired over-confidence in the opponent. He shoots, misses, curses, and you go on to win.

Of another species entirely is the Medical Pysche. Unlike the Rack Psyche, it can never be used among friends, unless they have been apart for more than six or eight months, have had no communication whatsoever, and have just suddenly found themselves beamed down into a pool hall somewhere, cues in hands, the break already made. The best Medical Pysche I have ever been the victim of involved a wiry toothless gentleman in a small neighborhood saloon called Niles Hay's in the village of Madeira, Ohio, in the 1970s. Madeira is a clean, interstate-accessed and upscale suburb of Cincinnati, with an inordinate number of brick ranches, Mercedes Benzes, and Powdermilk Biscuit children. It also happens to be where Joe Enzweiler spent most of his formative years, his family having moved from the countryside to Madeira in his youth.

The toothless man appeared inebriated when he staggered over to the table soon after I started to practice, and I saw that in addition to his absent dentition, he was also short an arm. I was wary of the apparent drunk, though — the type is guilty of the majority of attempted hustles, which even the greenest bumpkin soon learns to avoid.

"Hey!" this fellow shouted, waving his arm and leaning weirdly against the head of the table. "I'll shoot you a game. One-handed. You win, I buy you a beer. I win, you buy me one."

Now the Medical Psyche, properly played, involves a mixture of guilt, pathos, and opportunism. Guilt as in, "Oh this poor guy needs someone to shoot with him, and I'll bet no one will, what with his condition and all." Pathos as in, "What if I were disabled as he is. Wouldn't I want someone to play against, rather than suffer shunning? " Opportunism as in, "Oh here's some fool who's lost an arm. Thinks he can pysche me, but I'll be happy to take his beer, Oh yes thank you yes I will."

It was over in less than three minutes. I broke and sank a ball, then missed. The old man staggered off his stool and, barely able to stand upright, promptly ran the table. He lay his cue down carefully on the felt and turned his back to me with a mixture of dismissal and disdain. When I bought him his beer he refused to look at me. My own wits were uncollectible: there I was by the bar, sheepishly grinning; there I was at the entrance to the john, scratching my head; there I was by the front door, staring confusedly into my wallet. I hadn't gotten beaten, not even whipped: I had suffered the billiardistic equivalent of kidnapping by aliens who then operated on me in their spaceship as it hovered forty miles above Fort Wayne. I was a *National Enquirer* headline.

And so it was at the Crossroads that night with Jim Quinlivan. Shorty and Bent had won; I scratched on the eight ball. Now Shorty stood before me. I reached into what I thought might be my pocket and took out what I thought might be money and threw it down on what I thought might be the table. There was a pause during which I seemed to fall asleep and wake up again three or four times, and then there was this:

"What about the *other* five dollars?"

Ah. The "No, We Played For Five Dollars *Each* Pysche."

Now, I am not very brave. I didn't grow up in Steubenville for naught. How could any reasonably sensitive person brought up there escape a kind of chronic hypersensitivity to fear? My earliest memories are of skies glowing at night, hellish with millfires; of every hour of sleep interrupted by the prolonged shrill whining that preceded the explosion and roaring hiss of a blast furnace being tapped—all this at the height of the Cold War so that I was nightly convinced of the approach of Russian missiles, and clenched my eyes tight against the glare of the blast; of the six-foot catfish in the river that waited to gulp me down like an overgrown smelt; of the coal miners riding by in a car with their carbides like Cyclops' eyes; of the strange insects in the woods, like Ichneumon; of the dark tightnesses of Fox's Den, a cave over the hill from my house where as boys we wedged our ways so deeply into its sandstone crannies we had to let all the air out of our lungs to make it through, and where, sometimes, stuck for a moment, the first hum of panic arose in our cells.

I was not about to let Shorty rev that panic up again. Suddenly, the foggy drunkenness lifted for a moment: the landscape looked clear, precise, familiar. I was back in control; I knew exactly what to do.

"Less fie frit, den," I suavely said to him, who had again begun wavering liquidly in the air before me. Not only was my bladder failing, but language, too, was abandoning me. "Da fie dolls—

less fie frit, rie outsie," and I showed him the way to the door.

The rest of what must have been only thirty or forty seconds is, in memory now, a series of curiously frozen moments which only grudgingly thaw to slow motion when I concentrate: Shorty is in my face, his belly pushing against mine, and I am, I think, pirouetting madly as he tries to punch me. Then I am standing still, though I think Bent—or is it Shorty?—is leaning into me like the highwall of a mine slowly caving in, while directly behind him, Jim Quinlivan is backed against the pool table and in his right hand he is holding a longneck like a club and he is shouting, "Tell this Neanderthal to back off me!" Then, swiftly, I am on the floor looking for my glasses, knocked there, I think, by a thundering overhand right from Shorty, and a guy in blue jeans and an oxford cloth shirt kindly leans over from a bar stool and says, "They went that way," and I thank him kindly and crawl across the floor and there they are, leaning like a couple of flashlight lenses against the wall. Then I am trying to back my pickup out of the lot, but somehow I can't get it to turn. Jim is next to me, commenting, and I see out the windshield that it is very foggy and intensely dark, and I stop trying and I say, "You drive."

At one point—I don't know how many seconds or hours later—a horned owl comes suddenly up into the headlights out of the fog and at another Jim asks whether to turn right or left. What do I know? The only things at all clear in my otherwise addled mind are Thoreau's dying words: *Moose*. Then, a little later: *Indian*. The rest is silence.

Six

We found it impossible, of course, to continue the journey we had set out upon. We had planned to travel on to Williamson, West Virginia, and to the famous tavern and pool hall thereabouts known as the Red Robin Inn. Our friend Jim "Ski King" Webb, at that time a resident of Williamson, and its unofficial poet-in-residence, was to be our guide, and we had looked forward to getting down into his part of the country for some poetry, pool, and the related arts. (Jim was a main force in the publishing of a chapbook entitled "Mucked" which appeared after the Buffalo Creek disaster in the early 1970s, which had nothing to do with poolshooting—the disaster I mean—but a lot to do with pool shooters and their kin all over that region, rendered homeless by the mud and water.)

Had we gotten down to Williamson that day, it might have gone something like this: Jim Quinlivan and I would have driven through Williamson a couple of times looking for pool halls and taverns, and then, having gotten the lay of the land, we would have hunted up the Ski King's house. There, depending on the time, and how his business had gone the night before, we might have found him abed, his room warehousing such Webbian items as five dozen Baber Mountain Ramp Fest and Poultry Reading T-shirts, a dozen or so ballcaps with strings of flashing lights attached to them, a carton of uncirculated, mint condition 1955 Lava Lamps, eight flame pink yard flamingos, a copy or two of the literary magazine *What's A Nice Hillbilly Like You* and an audio tape of Jean-Paul Sartre reading from *No Exit*, alternating with Patsy Cline singing "I Fall To Pieces."

And then, after rousing the Ski King with a few lies and maybe a line or two of choice verse — *Obladi oblada, life goes on, braa* — maybe — we might have walked downtown and had a grilled cheese and a chocolate shake at the local drugstore, and admired the woman behind the counter with the strong chin and straight nose and hair the color of the air at twilight in a meadow of glowing broom sedge, and then we would have decided it was time to go have a few at the Red Bird, having taken our tonic of food, beauty, and dream for the day.

Ski King and I go a long way back, though not exactly together. When I was a boy growing up in Steubenville, Ski was a boy growing up in Shadyside, Ohio, just down the river. Had I known it then, I would have gotten my dad to drive me down there so I could meet the guy I would grow up to drink beer with and do poetry with and good-naturedly abuse later on. But life has a way of taking its own course, and thank goodness. For had I known that Ski King was to be a part of my life as an adult, I would never have volunteered for altar boys, nor said my prayers, nor would I have felt bad when Sr. Mary Isidore got blind-sided while supervising a recess football game in the playground that day at St. Peter's, and lay on the blacktop like a stunned saint, only her lips moving, which formed the words of some silent ejaculation or incantation that, I was sure, would levitate her to her feet unharmed. I would never have believed half the stuff I believed as a kid, had I known that Ski King would be there, twenty or thirty years alter, putting it all to the lie. "A person has got to have a job," they told us as kids—and it indeed seemed as if that were true. My dad worked, my grandfather worked, my uncles all worked, my grown-up cousins worked, even many mothers worked. But had I known Ski King then, I would have been able to tell them all happily that there was an alternative, another way.

"Dad, Mom. There's this guy I'm going to get to know in twenty-two or twenty-three years who was never an altar boy, who shot pool as a tot, and who, when he grew up, didn't work for almost a decade, not at any regular kind of job, and who was perfectly happy to do so."

"Yes, that's what we call a bum. You'll meet a lot of them in your life if you don't work hard in school and eat your peas."

"No. The Ski King is a genius, not a bum."

"What the hell kind of name is that, anyway—*Ski King*?

"It's a long story, but I don't know it yet."

"What you don't know won't hurt you. Now be quiet and do your subtraction."

But I think I know what it would have been like had Jim Quinlivan and I gone down there. Ski would have told us three or four stories, some true, about the place as we drove over to the Red Robin. When we walked in, two or three fellows at the bar would have turned in their stools and greeted us: "Gentlemen. Ski King."

Ski would have replied, "Now I didn't come in here just to be made sport of."

To which one of the fellows would have replied, "Well, where do you usually go?"

It would continue like that for five or ten minutes until the insults and wisecracks were done with; among the old Danes and Swedes of *Beowulf* fame, there was a similar ritual, called a *flyting*, in which a hired man of the king abused any stranger who showed up at court, questioning his manhood, suggesting his fame was undeserved, and so on. It was all a way of testing the mettle of the newcomer, of seeing what he was made of and how he'd reply. The poor sap who got the job when Beowulf showed up at Hrothgar's hall was named Unferth; Beowulf fielded his insults and then, steely and savage, turned them back on him.

There at the Red Bird it would have gone similarly. The Ski King would have parried the worst of them, and then good-naturedly railed at the "sorry varlets" who ruined his waking hours, and then he and Jim and I would have gotten on with our catching up and then a little later fed the jukebox for some Patsy Cline, during which Ski would fill us in on his latest part-time employment, which involved, over the years, everything from t-shirt entrepeneurship to Michigan Christmas trees to selling hats and other apparel decorated with flashing lights.

And then, outside a few beers each, we would have stood up and walked slowly over to the pool table, and slid a couple of quarters on the rail, and the evening would have then begun, right there on the Ski King's own home green.

Seven

My wife and I bought a century-old house in the early 1980s in Madisonville, a frontier settlement near Cincinnati which became a part of the city in the early 20th century. The second or third summer we were there, Ski King came north for a visit. By then he was living on Pine Mountain in Eastern Kentucky, near Whitesburg, and he was in and out of work. I was painting the trim on our house at the time: three big doorways with transoms, about 140 feet of wooden box gutter and crown molding, and 28 huge double-hung windows. The Ski had offered to help me whenever I set out to paint the place, so I had called him and here he was. We worked a week together scraping and priming and painting, and when it was all over, I asked him what I could give him for his help.

In the loft of the garage, where we had kept some of the painting supplies, I had stored my old canoe, an eighteen-and-a-half-foot Moore's Canadian, veteran of several voyages, including a 100-mile Ohio River float by Jim Quinlivan and me in the summer of 1978. Because of its size, the boat really required two people to handle it, so I hadn't used it much since starting serious work on the house. I don't think it had been in the water for more than a year by then. So when the question of pay came up and Ski said, "How about you give me the canoe?" I was willing to consider it. I felt bad about that noble craft, stored in a garage loft full of hornets and cat piss; it was an undignified confinement, and I was perpetrating it.

Many years ago, the poet Robert Graves presented a talk at which Joseph Wood Krutch, the essayist, was present. It was entitled "On The Word *Baraka*," and Krutch reports, "It turned out that this word is Arabic and refers to that particular charm (in both the literal and figurative sense of the word) which adheres to anything from a cooking pot to a mosque that has been long used either by an individual or his clan. Mr. Graves's point was that we rarely keep anything, cooking pot or building, long enough for it to acquire even a trace of this charm and that the central fact of our civilization is that we prefer newness to *baraka.*"

I knew what he meant. Maybe it's genetic, but my grandfather, when he was still alive, and now my father and I, are inveterate hoarders, pack rats, curators of informal collections of the strange, the fragrantly ancient, the off-the-wall, or as it sometimes turns out, the on-the-wall. Right next to the pool table in my basement is a wall covered with relics of one sort or another, all of which have *baraka.* They include a stylized but oddly animated representation of an elk, done in pencil and aluminum paint on unfinished plywood by my father at some point when he had too little paint left after a project to do anything else, but too much merely to throw away. He found a dandy wooden frame somewhere and gave the whole shebang to me, and I am grateful for it. How many can say they own a painting by their father? And this elk—it's a funny elk, spritely, on the move, vigorous and in its prime and a spontaneous work of art by a man who would consider himself the opposite of an artist, if pressed. It hangs just below two Yukon license plates which Joe brought back, and my 1963 blue and white Ohio motorcycle license plate, to which great sorrowful stories are attached. Let it be enough now to say that it was a Harley Davidson 125 with windshield and saddle seat and wide tires, and that I spent a week painting it Chinese Red, and that I rode it for three breathless days before being arrested. Next to that is the red-painted lid of my grandfather's toolbox (actually, there were two of them, one red and one green, as in the signals on the railroad), and it has his name *J C Hague* on it in jigsawed plywood letters.

This item exudes *baraka,* and by its very power and antiquity will survive the destruction of my house, however and whenever that comes. Next to it is a Stihl chainsaw advertising calendar, the kind you see in tree-trimmer's offices or car-repair shops. It features a dozen photos of European maidens occupying, in various states of deshabille, a room or exterior setting in the company of some Stihl product: there is, for example, the exhausted blonde leaning over a well somewhere in what must be the south of

France, and, lying in the background, as if the lover she has just arisen from, lolls a gas-powered weedeater, presumably just now cooling off, as in some kinkily literal re-enactment of the Virgin and the Dynamo. In between the toolbox lid and the calendar lurk the most dangerous relics of all: wallet-sized, brilliantly colored photographs—in official High Revolutionary style, of Che Guevara and Fidel Castro. Incredibly, Joe carried these photos in his wallet for almost two decades—decades during which he drove from Alaska to Ohio and back at least five times, through some of the least liberal landscape of America. I asked him one evening, "Joe, what would have happened if you'd broken down out in the boonies somewhere, and some good old boy stopped to help you? What if, for some reason, your wallet had flopped open, and he'd caught a load of those pictures? You might have been left to freeze outside Spearfish, or been left to the wolves at Delta Junction." He just grinned and reminded me, "The world is large."

All of these items were kept, of course, because they had *baraka*. My pool table itself, over which these things presided, has it, too. I bought the table for fifty dollars from my wife's business partner, who had kept it in his cellar. There, over the years, its plywood bed got so warped that Joe and I dubbed the right side pocket "The Black Hole" because of its propensity to swallow anything that passes by even vaguely near it on the table. Speaking physics once again, I have to report that in the region of the Black Hole, the ball enters a kind of trough or depression into which any passing thing—planet, satellite, eight ball on its way to the called corner pocket—is inexorably drawn, as surely as a ball bearing disappears when dropped down a flushing toilet.

All this only increases its *baraka* for us. We know the table's quirks like a lover might know his beloved's. We put up with it; we even celebrate it; this is its charm.

So it was a hard call—a very hard call—when Ski King allowed as how he might take that canoe, and all its accumulated *baraka,* in payment for helping me paint. Its *baraka* was of the most extraordinary kind, even though the craft was not that old. Its experience, as someone has put it, was to be measured not by its duration but by its intensity. That canoe had carried Jim Quinlivan and me into one of the adventures of our lives; it had been home to us for the better part of eight summer days through thunder and wind and nightfall and fog. We had seen that canoe like a golden sliver from an altitude of two thousand feet when a fellow whose patch of riverside meadow we'd camped on one of the nights on the trip came down the next morning and asked us if we wanted to take a little spin, and we hadn't known that he'd meant in his plane. And we had been in that canoe the day Elvis Presley died. We had gone ashore at Patriot, Indiana to stretch our legs and grab a snack and saw that all the waitresses were crying, and that people on the street stood leaning into their cars, listening to the radios that had already, in a spasm of technological grief, begun to play Elvis tunes uninterruptedly for the rest of the day.

So it was hard, thinking about all that charm and significance and personal association given up. But in as much as I was not able to take the boat out that whole domestic and busy summer, and as it was wasting away in the loft of the garage, I agreed. It was a comic sight to see an eighteen-and-a-half-foot canoe lashed to the top of a yellow Volkswagen Beetle, but then comedy is one of the Ski King's strengths. He claims the boat made the trip to Pine Mountain in one piece, but I recall shorter voyages when it went airborne off my truck and came skidding to a landing, most memorably skating for a hundred yards along Kentucky Route 8, so becoming the only canoe to have had both the river and river road beneath its hull on the same day.

In Eastern Kentucky, it accrued even more *baraka*, and the story of its premature and tragic demise there is a classic of unlikely Webbiana. Ski King had floated one of the branches of the Kentucky River in it; whether with the original paddles or not, I couldn't say. Those Ski had forgotten to take with him, so on my next trip to Lexington that summer, I dropped them off during a party at Monroe and Daveena Sexton's house, thinking that the Ski might show up there sometime. How long those paddles stood in the Sexton house I do not know.

But I do know that in the meantime, the canoe, when not in use, reposed on two sawhorses set up just behind the Ski's house on Pine Mountain. There the steady mountain rains washed its hull clean, and I suppose that its impressive length and beautiful curves looked competent and at home there.

It was three or four years later when a series of forest fires struck Appalachia, and Pine Mountain did not escape. Ski was in Whitesburg when the news came that there was a fire on Pine Mountain; by the time he got home, it had burned out. But when he walked around back of his place, he could see how close a call it had been: the canoe now lay in blackened puddles on the ground between the saw horses, its fiberglass hull melted in the heat of the fire that had stopped no more than a few yards from the house.

I was stunned when Ski King told me what had happened. But there was a strange kind of symmetry in the life of that canoe: the Indiana factory it had been built in had burned, and the dealer I bought it from had pointed out that the molds for the Canadian had been destroyed; it was one of the last of its kind. Now it lay melted into Pine Mountain, only its aluminum thwarts left whole. Like a great shot in pool, it lived in memory only, the more vivid and dramatic for its being gone now, irretrievable, placeless outside a few people's minds.

And where has its *baraka* gone? Into this account of its history, I hope. Into Ski King's hoard of stories. Into maybe a dozen people's memories, where its power continues to build among networks of nerve cells there, participating in billions of accumulating transactions and transformations of memory, to come out in later years even more richly appointed, more significantly shaped, more illustrative of the human meanings it mysteriously accrues: a kind of pyschic *baraka*.

Eight

During one of my stints at the Farm, my dad came down for a visit. We decided to go into Woodsfield for supper, and we wound up at the Belmont Grille. There was a pretty decent pool table in the back of the place, right next to the dining area, so we shot a couple of games.

I'd never before shot pool with my father. It was a strange feeling. As I racked the balls while he selected a cue from the dozen lined against the wall, I wondered if he would have any skill at all. Images of T.R.'s came to mind, and of the boyish forbidden adventure in my high school days. For a moment I saw myself gushing a hilarious confession to my father over this table, exposing all the trips to T.R.'s, all the cigarettes sneaked, all the bootlegged beers in the alley behind the place before we went in, red-eyed and belching, among the mafiosi and hoods.

As my own father, fiftyish, hair thinning, chalked his cue, I wondered if I would try to psyche him, my own dad, or if he would grinningly run the table on me, or if I would even try to win. A confusion of possibilities rose up before me. I tightened up at the head of the table, frozen over the rail.

"What you waiting for? Go ahead and break." He leaned slightly on his cue. As I lined my break shot up, he said, "I think the last time I ever got drunk was in here, twenty years ago. We were working the Graysville Loop then, putting in cable. We were all staying over at the Pioneer Motel, and Gilles and them guys kept giving me beer and we kept shooting pool. It was awful," he said, and laughed.

Relieved, I broke. And as my father and I moved around the table in our dusty jeans and boots, memories and impressions thickened and flared. But through them all, one came into particular focus. A few years before, my father and mother and I had gone on a long driving tour of the South and West, from Steubenville to Cincinnati to Eureka Springs, Arkansas, and on to New Orleans, then Texas and Oklahoma, then to Kansas and Missouri. One of our destinations was the home of my dad's brother Jack, in St. Joseph, Missouri. I remember walking into their house and seeing, on the wall inside the front door, a beautiful instrument. My uncle noticed me staring and said, "That was your grandfather's mandolin."

I was startled. I had known my grandfather for twenty-five years before he died, a couple of years before that visit, and I had never had an inkling that he had played any instrument whatsoever. I had taken up the guitar when I was a teenager, around the time of my first visits to T.R.'s, and yet my grandfather had never said a thing, never asked to pick it up and thumb a chord.

To me, it was like discovering as an adult that you had a twin, or that your father wasn't really your father. My whole life with my grandfather had to be rearranged to let this new thing in. Hadn't he been increasingly hard of hearing, deafened by his own years on the railroad? Had I ever heard so much as a sung note from him in the hundreds of masses we'd gone to at St. Peter's? And wasn't he — Ironhead, damner of governors, distruster of authority, curser of commies — wasn't he a hard guy, immune to the softening influences of music?

I took the instrument in my hands and sat down on a bench in the hall. Carefully, I tried to tune from its slack strings a single chord that might, I almost feared, shatter the years and the death that stood now between us. The keys squeaked and the strings were rough with tarnish and rust. The roundness of the mandolin nestled easily in my lap, like the head of a baby. Finally, I tried a chord, and the tinny sharpness of it fled into the air before me. My father and uncle were talking out on the porch; I was alone with the mandolin, and its voice, and the voice of someone long ago, someone my age, singing "Wildwood Flower."

It changed everything. I would have to re-order that past I thought I had lived; I would have to somehow make way, among his lives as steam locomotive engineer, horse-tracker, sworn-off drinker, old-time river fisherman and hobnobber with cronies from another age and time, for my grandfather singing and playing this instrument which was, it seemed there in that hot St. Joe hallway, as delicate and pretty as a girl.

This all came back to me at the Belmont Grille, and as I looked over the table at my father, Ironhead's son, I saw that the luck of life for any man is to hang around long enough for such things as these to come clear for him. Had I run away angry from my father as a young man, I would never have seen him in this light, never have shot pool with him in the upland country we both loved, never have learned the humanity of Ironhead had we not roamed the Achafalaya River country and eaten fried catfish in the boondocks there together, not long after which I somehow wound up in that Missouri hallway with his father's mandolin in my lap.

Those couple of games of eight ball in Woodsfield were rituals of linkage and remembrance. Where my first pool had been experienced in rebellion and disobedience and fear, this now, richened with experience, reflection, and memory, healed the circle. Ironhead was there with us, with my father and me, out there in the hinterlands, and so were all the others, even those as yet unknown, unencountered, though already gathering in smoky bars and roadstops to step into my life and invite me to play the game.

Richard Hague with sons Patrick Cavanaugh Hague and Brendan
Thomas Hague (photo by Joe Enzweiler)

RICHARD HAGUE was born and raised in Steubenville, Ohio, in the
steel and coal region of the upper Ohio Valley. He graduated from Catholic
Central High School there, and from Xavier University in Cincinnati. For a
time he worked for the Penn Central Railroad and for the Wheeling Steel
Corporation.

Since 1969 he has taught at Purcell Marian High School in Cincinnati, chairing the English Department. He has also taught at Edgecliff College, Xavier University and at the Univesity of Louisville's Kentucky Institute for Arts in Education. He has been a staff member for the Appalachian
Writers Workshop in Hindman, Kentucky, and has served as a cooridnator
of the Southern Appalachian Writers Cooperative.

In the mid-seventies he lived alone for two summers on Greenbriar
Ridge outside Graysville, Ohio, as he says, "hobnobbing with storytellers,
foresters, redoubtable blacksnakes, liars, and ginseng-hunters, and estab-
lishing intimate relationships with chiggers, ticks, thunderstorms, and a 1975
short-bed Chevy pickup." He now lives in Madisonville, one of Cincinnati's
older neighborhoods, with his wife Pam Korte (a potter and teacher) and
their two sons Patrick and Brendan.

Hague's publications include *Ripening* (Ohio State University Press,
1984), *Possible Debris* (Cleveland State University Poetry Center, 1988),
Mill and Smoke Marrow (in *A Red Shadow of Steel Mills*, Bottom Dog
Press, 1991), and *A Bestiary* (Pudding House Publications, 1996). His personal essays and fiction have appeared widely, often featured in *Ohio* Magazine. His book of essays, included here, was a Finalist in the Associated
Writing Programs Award for Creative Nonfiction.